MESOPOTAMIAN HISTORY AND ENVIRONMENT

SERIES II
MEMOIRS IV

DATING THE FALL OF BABYLON

A REAPPRAISAL OF SECOND-MILLENNIUM CHRONOLOGY

(A JOINT GHENT-CHICAGO-HARVARD PROJECT)

by

H. GASCHE, J.A. ARMSTRONG, S.W. COLE
and V.G. GURZADYAN

Published by the University of Ghent and the Oriental Institute of the University of Chicago
1998

MESOPOTAMIAN HISTORY AND ENVIRONMENT

SERIES II

MEMOIRS

MESOPOTAMIAN HISTORY AND ENVIRONMENT

Editors :
L. De Meyer and H. Gasche

SERIES II
MEMOIRS

Communications for the editors should be addressed to :

MESOPOTAMIAN HISTORY AND ENVIRONMENT
University of Ghent
Sint-Pietersplein 6
B-9000 GHENT Belgium

MESOPOTAMIAN HISTORY AND ENVIRONMENT

SERIES II
MEMOIRS IV

DATING THE FALL OF BABYLON

A REAPPRAISAL OF SECOND-MILLENNIUM CHRONOLOGY

(A JOINT GHENT-CHICAGO-HARVARD PROJECT)

by

H. GASCHE, J.A. ARMSTRONG, S.W. COLE
and V.G. GURZADYAN

Published by the University of Ghent and the Oriental Institute of the University of Chicago
1998

Abbreviation of this volume : *MHEM* IV

D/1998/0634/1 (Belgium)
ISBN 1-885923-10-4 (USA)
Library of Congress Catalog Card Number : 98-84354

Printed in Belgium
The fonts used are based on CunéiTyp 1 designed by D. Charpin.

This volume presents research results of an 'Interuniversity Poles of Attraction Programme - Belgian State, Prime Minister's Office - Federal Office for Scientific, Technical and Cultural Affairs.'

CONTENTS

Fugit irreparabile tempus (Virgil, *Georgics*, III, 284)

PREFACE

This study has its genesis in a detailed examination of the pottery of Babylonia and adjacent regions in the second millennium BC.[1] As a result of that work we have been able to trace the evolution of Babylonian pottery and pottery technology during the second millennium. For the early second millennium, we can reconstruct a ceramic sequence representing the 400-year period between the fall of Ur under Ibbi-Sîn and the fall of Babylon under Samsuditana. We also have a detailed sequence for the fourteenth and thirteenth centuries and a twelfth-to-eleventh-century sequence that, even though it is less detailed due to a lack of excavated material, is nonetheless coherent. However, we are left with a gap of uncertain duration between the period of the fall of Babylon and the fourteenth century BC. The so-called Middle Chronology — the most frequently criticized, yet still the most frequently cited, of the three principal chronologies for the early second millennium BC — places the fall of Babylon in 1595 BC. If the Middle Chronology is correct, then about two centuries separated the fall of Babylon and the fourteenth century and about 200 years of the artifactual record must be accounted for in the data we have to work with. It is our contention that the similarities in form between the shapes belonging to the end of our early second-millennium sequence and those we date to the beginning of the fourteenth century do not allow for the intervention of so great a span of time.

The unresolved problem of the absolute chronology of the ancient Near East during the second millennium BC has vexed several generations of scholars, and a number of approaches have been attempted over the years to obtain a satisfactory solution. In the case of Mesopotamia the arguments until recently were adduced almost exclusively from written sources, with little or no reference to other archaeological data. This was not just a matter of neglect. Establishing the date of non-epigraphic materials has rarely been a simple or straightforward undertaking, and the end result has almost never had the precision needed to serve as the basis for absolute chronology. Moreover, besides the limitations inherent in the materials themselves, there were frequently also problems with the excavations that had produced them, excavations that were generally carried out with insufficient attention paid either to stratigraphical detail or to the retrieval and recording of archaeological materials. The information derived from such excavations has rarely been sufficiently conclusive or trustworthy to be of much use in discussions of chronology.

---

1 This study would not have been possible without the wholehearted support and cooperation of the following persons and institutions to whom we would like to extend our warmest thanks : L. De Meyer, K. Minsaer (Belgian Archaeological Expedition to Iraq) ; M. Gibson, J. Franke, R. Zettler (Oriental Institute, Nippur Expedition) ; R.McC. Adams (formerly Secretary of the Smithsonian Institution) ; B. Hrouda, K. Karstens, A. Hausleiter (University of Munich, Isin Exped.) ; J.-L. Huot, C. Kepinski-Lecomte, Y. Calvet, O. Aurenche (University of Paris I, C.N.R.S, Larsa, Khirbet ed-Diniyeh and Failaka Exped., and Maison de l'Orient, Lyon) ; A. Caubet, F. Tallon (Louvre) ; A. Invernizzi, G. Bergamini, E. Valtz (University of Turin, Yelkhi Exped. and Museo delle Antichità Egizie) ; D. Hansen, E. Ochsenschlager (New York Univ., al-Hiba Exped.) ; J.-C. Margueron (E.P.H.E., Mari Exped.), N. Pons (URA 1557, Strasbourg and Belgian Archaeol. Exped. to Iraq) ; W. Sallaberger (Univ. of Leipzig) ; and A. Van As, L. Jacobs (University of Leiden).

Therefore, the objective of the present study is to present a new, coherent scheme for Mesopotamian chronology during the second millennium. Because Susa is one of the few excavated sites that shows a continuity in occupation between the time of the fall of Babylon and c. 1400 BC and, in addition, yields ceramic information for the Babylonian corpus, we also connect the Elamite chronology with the Babylonian system of dating. On the other hand, although the absolute chronologies throughout the Ancient Near East are largely dependent on Babylonian data, they are given less consideration here because the archaeological evidence from these areas is only remotely related to that stemming from Mesopotamia and therefore lies outside the scope of this study.

In what follows we will : 1) review the problems associated with the reconstruction of the Mesopotamian chronology of the second millennium before the fourteenth century, 2) present the ceramic evidence that supports our contention that the Middle Chronology is too long, 3) examine the documentary evidence that can be brought to bear on the issue, and 4) introduce a new discussion of the astronomical evidence that until now has served as the starting-point for discussions of Mesopotamian chronology. We will establish that the ceramic evidence calls for a shortening of the traditional Middle Chronology dates on the order of a century. We will next show that the textual sources permit a reduction of some 85 to 105 years. Finally, because of this relatively narrow chronological range, we can assign astronomical phenomena such as lunar eclipses — recorded in ancient sources in association with known historical events — to definite calendar years.

This study has been a joint undertaking with each of the authors contributing in the area of his expertise : James A. Armstrong and Hermann Gasche in archaeology, Steven W. Cole in epigraphy, and Vahe G. Gurzadyan (Univ. of Sussex, UK ; Physics Inst., Erevan) in astronomy. The approach we have adopted here, which utilizes archaeological materials of both epigraphic and non-epigraphic character, takes advantage of recent advances in data retrieval in Mesopotamian archaeology and the consequent increase in the reliability and consistency of information. We believe that only with close cooperation between the distinct — but allied — disciplines of Assyriology and Mesopotamian archaeology can we hope to avail ourselves of the greater chronological precision also now afforded by recent advances in dating techniques made in the natural sciences. To collaborate on this level, however, it is essential that we communicate within the same chronological framework. For example, environmental researchers have been confronted with a significant difference between dates derived from historical chronologies and those evidenced by the physical dating techniques with which they primarily work. But now, because the chronology proposed here is anchored in absolute time, it offers the possibilty for specialists in the different disciplines to collaborate within better correlated systems.

Acknowledgements

We acknowledge with gratitude the support of L. De Meyer, M. Gibson, and P. Steinkeller in this undertaking. We also thank F. Vallat for his active collaboration and advice concerning chronological problems relating to Elamite-Mesopotamian interactions and O. Gingerich for his advice on ancient astronomical data, particularly the "Venus Tablet." We express our appreciation as well to G. Bergamini for discussing with us the excavations at Tell Yelkhi, and we thank M.S. Demerji and Nawala al-Mutawally for facilitating our examination of archaeological materials in the Iraq Musuem. We are also grateful to M. Gibson and M. Tanret for their constructive advice and C. Janssen for her helpful comments and Arabic translation.

We express, however, our most heartfelt gratitude to M.-J. Steve and J.A. Brinkman. They not only inspired our ideas and approach but also pointedly critiqued them. Without the help of J.A. Brinkman, in particular, we would not have been able to grasp all the complexities addressed herein. Nevertheless, all statements, interpretations, opinions, and conclusions expressed in this work are those of the authors alone.

The figures were produced by E. Smekens with his usual good humor, patience, and skill. Finally, we wish to thank Marie Boscals de Reals for her generous hospitality during several working sessions in Paris.

1.

Present Sources for the Chronology of the Second Millennium

1.1. Textual and Archaeological Evidence

The chronologies for the first and second halves of the second millennium are based upon two distinct, non-overlapping sets of documentary materials. The chronology for the latter half of the second millennium — more precisely, from around 1400 on — is secured ultimately by Assyrian chronological sources.[2] When taken together, these sources allow us to determine nearly absolute dates for Assyrian rulers beginning in the latter part of the fifteenth century, dates that are fixed by the mention, in the later Assyrian eponym chronicle, of a solar eclipse in the eponymy of Bur-Saggilê (reign of Aššur-dān III).[3] This eclipse has been calculated to have occurred exactly on 15 June 763 BC.[4] A complex matrix of synchronisms between Assyrian and Babylonian rulers provides the relatively secure Babylonian chronology for this period, with dates that are precise within two decades from around 1400 on.[5]

Before 1400, stretching back to the end of the reign of Samsuditana, the situation changes dramatically for the worse. The native Mesopotamian chronographic sources pertaining to this period — which consist mainly of chronicles and lists of kings and dynasties — pose a number of problems for the modern interpreter. Many are in fragmentary condition, giving rise to considerable disagreement among editors about readings. Moreover, the ancients sometimes seem to have assumed that dynasties and reigns were consecutive when they in fact overlapped.[6] Also, texts were sometimes copied from originals that were damaged already in antiquity.[7] Finally, in the rare cases where multiple written exemplars of a native chronological tradition actually exist, these exhibit

---

2 The Assyrian kinglists, the eponym lists, and the eponym chronicle. A good recent summary of the reliablity (and limitations) of the Assyrian chronological sources can be found in POSTGATE 1991.

3 See MILLARD 1994, 41.

4 See, for example, UNGNAD 1938b, 414 (with earlier literature); VAN DER MEER 1963, 6; and BRINKMAN 1968, 68.

5 BRINKMAN 1977, 335.

6 As in the Sumerian Kinglist and Babylonian Kinglist A.

7 As was the case in at least two Assyrian Kinglist manuscripts, where the ancient scribes have used the word *ḫīpu*, "break" (or *ḫepi*, "broken"), to indicate the presence of damage on the originals that they copied (see, for example, BRINKMAN 1973, 315). This was apparently also the case with the received text of Kinglist A, in which forty percent of the royal names appear in truncated form, probably indicating damage to the original (see, for example, GRAYSON 1980-83, 91; see also the remarks by BRINKMAN 1976, 426-427). The original of Babylonian Kinglist B was also broken (see FEIGIN and LANDSBERGER 1955, 140).

discrepancies.[8] In short, the textual sources for the period between the fall of Babylon and c. 1400 are scarce, non-contemporaneous, imperfectly preserved, of questionable reliability, and inconsistent with one another. It has thus far proved impossible to reconstruct definitively the chronology for this obscure period from such a basis.[9]

In contrast, the reign of Samsuditana marks the end of a more than 500-year-long block of time for which the internal chronology is relatively well fixed because of synchronisms. However, since the chronology of the post-Samsuditana period is unknown, the pre-Samsuditana period, comprising the dynasties of Babylon I, Larsa, Isin I, and Ur III, cannot be linked up directly with the chronology that prevails after 1400.

Investigators have therefore turned to the ancient astronomical records found in the so-called "Venus Tablet of Ammiṣaduqa" [10] for assistance. The "Venus Tablet," known only in copies from the seventh century and later, records astronomical observations placing Venus on the horizon [11] just prior to sunrise on the date of the new moon during the reign of Ammiṣaduqa.[12] On the assumption that these data are reliable, the Venus Tablet has been utilized to provide absolute dates for the succession of kings from the beginning of the Third Dynasty of Ur to the end of the First Dynasty of Babylon.

Unfortunately, the data of the Venus Tablet do not provide us with a single set of certain dates, but instead with several series of possible dates, the most frequently cited of which are the so-called "High" (or "Long"), "Middle," and "Low" (or "Short") Chronologies.[13] Scholars have chosen among the several potential chronologies generated by the Venus Tablet data based upon the relative weight they have assigned to other pieces of evidence, but they have still been unable convincingly to bridge the gap between the fall of the First Dynasty of Babylon and the more secure post-1400 chronology. According to the High Chronology, the final year of Samsuditana's reign was 1651 BC ; according to the Middle, 1595 ; and according to the Low, 1531.

Returning to the period following the fall of Babylon, we observe that the final years of Samsuditana's reign and the decades that followed are shrouded in almost complete darkness. There are virtually no contemporary sources on which to base either a solid historical reconstruction or a reliable chronology. Babylon seems to have fallen to the Hittite king Muršili I [14] in a raid known to us from an inscription of Telepinu, who ruled the Hittites perhaps as much as a century after the event. The collapse of Samsuditana's rule is assumed to have been the result of this raid, although these two events are nowhere directly connected in ancient sources. Confirmation of Babylon's fall in Babylonian records comes only in later copies of inscriptions of questionable authenticity and in

---

8 See, for example, BRINKMAN 1973, 311-314.

9 BRINKMAN 1976, 75-78.

10 The most recent full publication is REINER and PINGREE 1975.

11 For an illustration of this phenomenon, see Pingree in REINER and PINGREE 1975, fig. 1 on p. 16.

12 REINER and PINGREE 1975.

13 Less frequently cited are an "Ultra-high" and an "Ultra-low" Chronology.
For an overview of all these chronologies, see the selected bibliography assembled by CAMPBELL 1979, to which may be added ROWTON 1976. See also, now, ÅSTRÖM (Ed.) 1987, HUBER *et al.* 1982, and HUBER 1987a.

14 HOFFMANN 1984, 18-19 ; cf. also HOFFNER 1975, 56-58.

later traditions. Thus, in the late Chronicle of Early Kings we are told that in the time of Samsuditana, the Hittites marched against the land of Akkad.[15] A possible school text of the first millennium, if authentic and interpreted correctly, seems to refer to a temple restoration by the first Kassite ruler, Gandaš, after his conquest of Babylon.[16] A seventh-century copy of what purports to be a royal inscription of Agum-kakrime records that this ruler, whose name is not preserved in the kinglists in this form, returned the statues of Marduk and Zarpanītum to Babylon [17] from the land of Ḫani,[18] where they were presumably left by Muršili I. Finally, the late "Marduk Prophecy" refers to Marduk's 24-year sojourn in Ḫatti, a presumed reference to these same events.[19]

The uncertainty of any reconstruction based on such evidence is apparent. The poverty of documentary sources for the rest of this obscure period is, if anything, even greater until Babylonia reemerges into relative light around 1400.[20]

Not coincidentally, archaeologists have had a difficult time identifying post-Old Babylonian levels on Babylonian sites. One reason for this is that the principal Old Babylonian sites — certainly those that have been most thoroughly excavated — were largely, if not completely, abandoned either during or at the end of the Old Babylonian Period. This process began well before the collapse of the First Dynasty of Babylon. Already by Samsuiluna year 10, about 140 years before the end of the reign of Samsuditana, urban centers in southern Babylonia began to be abandoned and the region passed out of the control of the Babylonian crown. Some data suggest that this was in part due to the loss of water in the branches of the Euphrates that served the southern and central parts of the country.[21] This process of deurbanization first struck, among others, the Euphrates cities of Ur, Uruk, and Larsa. Girsu and Lagaš, situated on the eastern side of the Šaṭṭ al-Ġarrāf, and therefore apparently at least partially dependent upon the Tigris for water,[22] were also

---

15 GRAYSON 1975, 156, rev. 11.

16 BRINKMAN 1976, 127, H.3.1. WEIDNER (1957-71) asserts that the conquest of Babylon is not mentioned in this text.

17 BRINKMAN 1976, 97, D^b.3.1.

18 PINCHES 1880, Pl. 33 col. ii 9. It is uncertain whether the land of Ḫani mentioned in this text is the same as the land of Ḫana on the Middle Euphrates.

19 BORGER 1971, 5, col. i 13-17.

20 Even though they were found in later archaeological contexts, two inscriptions from the post-Old Babylonian Period, each bearing the name "Ula-Burariaš, son of Burna-Burariaš," should be mentioned here: 1) a knob or macehead from a Parthian jeweller's hoard at Babylon that identifies Ula-Burariaš as "king of the Sealand" (WEISSBACH 1903, 7 and Pl. 1, No. 3), and 2) a frog-shaped shekel-weight found in an eleventh-ninth century BC (pers. comm. E. Khanzadyan) burial at Metsamor, Armenia that identifies Burna-Burariaš, father of Ula-Burariaš, as "king" (KHANZADYAN 1983; SARKISYAN and DIAKONOFF 1983). Ula-Burariaš apparently ruled as king of the Sealand at some point after the fall of Babylon, but he is not known to have ruled as king of Babylon (BRINKMAN 1976, 318-319).

21 GASCHE (1989b, 111-143) presents the basic data for the progressive abandonment of southern Babylonia in the Old Babylonian Period. He observes (1989b, 140-141) that when the south was experiencing a water crisis there were also serious inundations in northwestern Babylonia. For Nippur, see STONE 1977; GIBSON 1980, 199-200; and ARMSTRONG and BRANDT 1994. ADAMS' survey data (1981, 165-168, figs. 33-34) suggest that canals in southern Babylonia were reoriented after the Old Babylonian Period in order to tap more westerly channels of the Euphrates for water.

22 The present flow of water in the Šaṭṭ al-Ġarrāf depends upon a barrage and regulator on the Tigris near Kūt, an arrangement that obviously does not reflect the situation in antiquity. The impressive natural levee on top of which the modern-day Šaṭṭ al-Ġarrāf meanders is clearly visible in satellite images (see also BURINGH 1960, map 1, where the first 40 km of this levee south of Kūt are shown), and is from all evidence the result of a large natural channel that carried a significant flow of water for centuries, if not for millennia. Although the possibility of a connection with a branch of the ancient Euphrates system has not yet been excluded, this channel most probably provided Girsu and Lagaš with water from the Tigris.

abandoned at this time. Some 20 years later, around Samsuiluna year 30, the central Babylonian cities of Isin and Nippur were lost. At that point things seem to have stabilized, and the urban centers of the more environmentally favored enclave of northwestern Babylonia continued to exist for another century or so. But, finally, during the reigns of Ammiṣaduqa and Samsuditana Babylon began to lose hydraulic, if not political, control over even this much diminished realm, and at least some of the northwestern cities were abandoned as well.

At Nippur [23] and at Tell ed-Dēr [24] (Sippar-Amnānum) layers of wind- and/or water-deposited soil have been identified between Old Babylonian and Kassite levels, indicating an interlude of abandonment in the occupation of at least a part of these cities. Based on published descriptions, similar deposits may also be present between Old Babylonian and Kassite layers at Larsa [25] and between Old Babylonian and Isin II layers at Isin.[26]

Among the Babylonian sites that have been adequately excavated and published, those that were subsequently resettled after being abandoned during the Old Babylonian Period were on present evidence reoccupied some time after the Kassites took control in Babylon.[27] As a result, excavated, published material from the alluvial plain that can be securely placed in the period immediately after the fall of Babylon is for the present essentially nonexistent.

In this context, we must mention F. Højlund's placement of archaeological remains from the Gulf in the post-Old Babylonian Period we have been discussing here.[28] While we do not argue with Højlund's basic division of his Kassite materials into earlier and later groups, his assignment of the earlier Kassite group to a span of time extending from the fall of Babylon to 150 years later has no firm basis in the Babylonian evidence he cites.

The earliest contemporary documentary sources for the Kassite Dynasty have been found at Uruk and Nippur, and belong to a period beginning shortly before 1400.[29] From Uruk come building inscriptions of Kara-indaš,[30] all, unfortunately, recovered from secondary contexts.[31] Nippur

---

23 ARMSTRONG and BRANDT 1994.

24 GASCHE 1989b, 8-9 ; 1991, 24, 31.

25 PARROT 1968a, 213-14, 217 : fig. 9 ; PARROT 1968b, 40, fig. 4 ; GASCHE 1989b, 129, n. 358.

26 KARSTENS 1981, 39.

27 Levels that can be associated with the earliest years of Kassite rule at Babylon have yet to be identified in excavations at that site.

28 "Failaka 3B" and "Qala'at al-Bahrain IIIA," see HØJLUND 1987, 157-161 ; 1989 ; and HØJLUND and ANDERSEN 1997, 50-62.

29 J.A. Brinkman has kindly called our attention to a text from Nippur (2NT 356 = UM 55-21-62) recently published by SASSMANNSHAUSEN (1994), which may be the earliest Kassite text known from the site. It contains many nouns with mimation clearly expressed (and not just in CVC signs), with words showing initial *w*, and personal names without a preceding determinative. In I' 5' is a reference to a [-B]uriaš, perhaps a ruler or an official.

Unfortunately, the provenience of this document (Area TB Locus 62 [McCOWN and HAINES 1967, Pl. 65]) is poorly defined and potentially disturbed. It provides no information to help date this text or to relate it to other Kassite artifacts and contexts at Nippur. Therefore, we have been unable to incorporate it into our discussion of the evidence from Nippur bearing on the Early Kassite Period.

30 BRINKMAN 1976, 169-171, N.2.1-N.2.2.

31 SCHOTT 1930, 53-54, Texts 12-13.

The inscribed brick that was used to identify the so-called Kara-indaš Temple was found in debris about 50 m away (SCHOTT 1930, 53, Text 12). The bricks of the relief-facade, although they are certainly Kassite in date, were all found in secondary contexts as well (JORDAN 1930, 33). Nothing from the building itself, nor any other structure presently published from Uruk, can be definitively attributed to the period of Kara-indaš's reign.

has yielded a legal text dated to the reign of Kadašman-Ḫarbe I,[32] an economic text from the reign of Kurigalzu I,[33] and another legal document dated to the reign of either Kadašman-Ḫarbe I or Kadašman-Enlil I.[34] Because the findspots of these items from Nippur are not known, they cannot be used directly to date specific contexts at this site, but they do provide evidence of the settlement's existence at the end of the fifteenth century.

The earliest Kassite levels from recent excavations have been found at Nippur [35] and Tell ed-Dēr.[36] We have dated these contexts from Nippur and Tell ed-Dēr to the fourteenth and late fifteenth centuries ; some material from Tell ed-Dēr seems to be slightly earlier.[37] The artifacts from these levels and the issues surrounding their date will be discussed in detail in Chapter 2.

As can be seen, excavations in Babylonia have thus far failed to provide the resources necessary for a definitive reconstruction of the chronology, history, or archaeology of the period between the end of the First Dynasty of Babylon and about 1400, largely because of a widespread interruption in settlement. The shortest post-Old Babylonian gap known from published excavations is at Tell ed-Dēr. This hiatus begins around Ammiṣaduqa year 18, and as we shall argue in Chapter 2, extends to sometime in the latter half of the fifteenth century.

1.2. ASTRONOMICAL EVIDENCE

Ancient astronomical records offer the tantalizing possibility of determining precise dates in antiquity. Thus the observations recorded in the Venus Tablet have been used repeatedly to establish the chronology of the early second millennium. Indeed, if the data preserved therein were more complete and exhibited fewer corruptions, they would provide a compelling chronological argument. However, the data in the texts are incomplete and not totally reliable, as others have already asserted.[38] On the other hand, P.J. Huber has argued that, in spite of the problems with the Venus Tablet data, it is possible to extract statistically significant information from them.[39] He has concluded that the High Chronology is the most probable of the three traditional alternatives. However, he did not take into account the existence of other possibilities. The extent to which the Venus Tablet data can be used is considered below in Chapter 4. The conclusion reached there is that the only reliable chronological information that can be derived from the Venus Tablet is that year 1 of

32 BRINKMAN 1976, 146, K[a].2.1 ; 388, Text 18.

33 BRINKMAN 1976, 239-240, Q.2.115.168, and p. 402, published later by DONBAZ 1987, D. 85.

34 BRINKMAN 1976, 144, J.5.5 ; 391, Text 23.

35 FRANKE 1978, 80-81, fig. 66, 1-4 ; GIBSON 1978a, 12-13 ; fig. 19, 1 and 3 ; ARMSTRONG 1993, 75. On the basis of further work with the second-millennium pottery, we believe that the published dating of the early Kassite levels at Nippur to "as early as the latter part of the fourteenth century," (*ibid.*) is too conservative. This pottery may well be earlier in date. This matter will be discussed in greater detail below in Section 2.2.

36 PONS 1989, 22-23 ; GASCHE 1991 ; MINSAER 1991.

37 Especially the grave goods from Burial 392 found in Operation F (PONS 1989, 22-23, Pl. 5).

38 REINER and PINGREE 1975, 25.

39 HUBER *et al.* 1982 ; HUBER 1987a ; 1987b.

Ammiṣaduqa must be identified with a year in which the Venus phenomenon (recurring every eight years) took place.[40]

Records of lunar eclipses also appear in ancient sources, and these have been used in the past to provide possible confirmation for chronological schemes based on the Venus observations.[41] Lunar eclipses, of course, occur comparatively frequently, and one needs to define as closely as possible the most likely time range before attempting to identify particular occurrences. This we have tried to do in the case of two Ur III eclipses, without first assuming that only the three traditional Venus Tablet-based chronological schemes are possible ; the results of this investigation also appear in Chapter 4.

1.3. RELEVANT PHYSICAL TECHNIQUES FOR ESTABLISHING AN ABSOLUTE CHRONOLOGY

Physical techniques, including ^{14}C dating and dendrochronology, appear to offer assistance in establishing an absolute chronology for historical periods like the one under examination here.[42] Advances in ^{14}C techniques in recent years have substantially narrowed the standard deviation to just a few decades.[43]

In the field of dendrochronology, P. Kuniholm has established a tree-ring sequence for central Anatolia that covers the end of the third millennium, the entire second millennium, and the beginning of the first, for a total of 1503 years.[44] As of 1996, this sequence was fixed in terms of absolute dates by means of high-precision ^{14}C determinations, with a confidence error of +76/-22 calendar years.[45]

Kuniholm has used his dendrochronological sequence to date the timbers of a large building at Acemhöyük.[46] This building, referred to as the Sarıkaya Palace, contained bullae that were impressed with the seal of Šamšī-Adad I.[47] The sequence is thereby linked to a well-known historical figure, whose dates relative to those of the First Dynasty of Babylon can be figured fairly closely. Kuniholm's analysis indicates that the timbers used in the palace were felled in 1752 BC (+76/-22).[48] Even the highest date represented by the margin of error, 1828 BC, is still almost a decade later than the traditional date of Šamšī-Adad I's death according to the High Chronology, 1837 BC. While it is not impossible for bullae impressed with a ruler's seal to be found in a

40 That is, it must be a multiple of 8 years subtracted from, or added to, 1646, the date of year 1 of Ammiṣaduqa according to the Middle Chronology.

41 For example, HUBER 1987a.

42 For other techniques, e.g. archaeomagnetic dating, thermoluminescent dating of pottery, fission track dating, and obsidian hydration dating, and their limits, see, for example, MICHAEL and RALPH (Ed.) 1973.

43 For a good explanation of how the radiocarbon method and its interpretation work, see MANNING 1995.

44 KUNIHOLM 1993 ; KUNIHOLM *et al.* 1996.

45 KUNIHOLM *et al.* 1996, 780.

46 KUNIHOLM 1993, 372.

47 KUNIHOLM (1993, 372) attributes one bulla to the tenth year of Šamšī-Adad I ; however, the basis upon which he arrives at this date is unclear. Bullae are rarely if ever dated, and the sequence of the eponyms corresponding to the reign of Šamšī-Adad has not yet been definitely established.

48 KUNIHOLM *et al.* 1996, 782.

building erected after that ruler's death, the circumstantial evidence in this case tends to support the conclusion that a chronology shorter than the High Chronology is preferable.

Nevertheless, in utilizing dendrochronological or, for that matter, ^{14}C evidence, one must deal with the critical question concerning when the botanical or zoological remains entered the archaeological record and the temporal relationship between them and the other artifacts found in the same context. This limitation is especially significant when architectural members are used for purposes of dating, whether by ^{14}C or dendrochronology, because the span of time separating the felling of the timbers and their final deposition in the archaeological record is undeterminable.

While we recognize the great potential importance of these techniques for chronological investigations, they unfortunately have been able to contribute little information to the present undertaking.

2.

The Archaeological Evidence

Introduction

Until now the analysis of archaeological materials from Babylonia has played almost no role in the debate over second-millennium chronology. This has been true partly because of the pre-eminence of the written documents for dating purposes and partly because of the inadequacy of the available archaeological data.

The archaeological data have been insufficient because the relevant periods have frequently not been represented in the sites that have been excavated and because the excavation techniques generally in use in southern Iraq until recently have been inadequate to permit the clean separation of materials from different stratigraphic contexts. Such techniques are an essential precondition for the development of sound, stratigraphically-based arguments. More recent excavations in southern Iraq have begun to address the earlier shortcomings and are more frequently characterized by better stratigraphic control and by an emphasis on the recovery and registration of as much of the archaeological record as possible, in particular, the ceramics — not only whole vessels, but also potsherds ; not only the fine and decorated wares, but the common wares too. Thus, data have begun to be recorded that permit the observation of the gradual evolution in the shapes of vessels and in the techniques used in their manufacture, especially in the case of those that were produced in large quantities.

These advances have helped make possible the general study of second-millennium Babylonian pottery that underlies the present investigation. The goal of this general study has been to create a regional corpus of ceramic shapes arranged according to the two axes of space and time. We have focused especially on the shapes that were the most commonly produced, because the absence of otherwise common shapes at a given site or a given point in time is most likely to be of geographical and/or temporal significance. On the other hand, shapes that occur infrequently, even if they are interesting aesthetically or otherwise, are less useful for such comparisons because the significance of their absence from a particular context is very difficult to assess.

The chronological framework underlying the second-millennium corpus, the temporal axis, has been provided principally by the stratigraphic sequences at Tell ed-Dēr and Nippur. We relied on these sites mainly because each has a relatively long archaeological sequence for the second millennium, whose excavation has been the objective of recent campaigns.[49] In addition,

49 Tell ed-Dēr from 1970 to 1989 and Nippur from 1972 to 1990.

considerable attention has been paid by both projects to the stratigraphic analysis of the excavated ceramic material. The two sites are about 140 km apart, with Tell ed-Dēr (Sippar-Amnānum) situated in the Northern Alluvial Plain and Nippur at the northern end of the Southern Alluvial Plain.[50] The distance between the two sites is reflected in the differences in their ceramic assemblages.

The spatial component of the corpus has been augmented by material from shorter, less complete sequences at Tell ed-Deylam [51] (Dilbat) in northern Babylonia and Isin, Larsa, Uruk, and Lagaš in the South. With the exception of the sequence at the Sinkašid Palace at Uruk, the material from Babylonian sites that we have used for the corpus has usually, though not exclusively, come from relatively recent excavations, in some cases still unpublished. We have drawn upon the information from these sites — Tell ed-Dēr, Nippur, and the others — in order to define our corpus of shapes that were produced and were in general use in Babylonia, here defined as the alluvial plain between the Tigris and Euphrates, south of Baghdad.

Expanding beyond the limits of the alluvial plain of lower Mesopotamia, we have also examined material belonging to the Babylonian ceramic tradition in the adjacent regions, where other pottery traditions are also present. To the northwest, Khirbet ed-Diniye (Ḫarādum) in the Ḥadīṯa salvage area along the Middle Euphrates has provided an assemblage dated to the latter part of the Old Babylonian Period, down to the reign of Ammiṣaduqa. In the Diyala Basin to the north and northeast, the salvage sites excavated during the late 1970s in the Hamrin Project Area have proved to be a rich resource for comparative material, especially the late second-millennium levels at Zubeidi and Imlihiye, and the longer stratigraphic sequence at Yelkhi. To the east and southeast, relevant ceramics come from older excavations in the Susiana Plain. Of these, Susa is especially important in the present case, because there is no stratigraphic rupture in Operation A of the Ville Royale during the years following the downfall of the First Dynasty of Babylon, a time of significant deurbanization in Babylonia. Finally, to the south there are the sites in the Gulf, principally on the islands of Bahrain and Failaka, where Babylonian material from several periods in the second millennium has been excavated. Except for the Gulf, we have utilized material from sites in each of the above-mentioned regions in the present, chronologically oriented study.

The most significant site whose finds have not been utilized is Babylon, the chief city of Babylonia in all the periods being studied here. One can only regret the lack of archaeological precision in the excavation of the remains at Babylon from the period that immediately preceded and followed the end of the First Dynasty of Babylon. The remains of houses excavated by the Germans on the mound of Merkes between 1907 and 1912 could be dated to the time of Samsuditana by the texts that were found in them.[52] However, the few pottery vessels from these structures that were published are not diagnostic for the end of the Old Babylonian Period.[53] Moreover, the ceramics

50 The terms Northern and Southern Alluvial Plain more-or-less correspond respectively to the Flood Plain and the Delta Plain of Southern Iraq as described by BURINGH 1960, 143-184.

51 Modern geographical names are transcribed with the appropriate diacritics except those in common usage (Baghdad, Diyala, etc.). Most names of archaeological sites are transcribed according to the usage of the excavators.

52 REUTHER 1926, 4, 7. The latest published Old Babylonian text from Babylon bears the date Samsuditana year 26 (or 27) (KLENGEL 1983, No. 77).

53 REUTHER 1926, fig. 1, 2. For the characteristic pottery profiles from the end of the Old Babylonian Period, see GASCHE 1989b, 97-98 ; certain of these forms are attested in contemporary remains at Tell ed-Deylam (unpublished) and at Kish, see, for example, DE GENOUILLAC 1925, Pl. XVIII : 1, lower row, center.

from the remains found immediately above those of the period of Samsuditana already must be assigned to a relatively late stage in the Kassite Period.[54] Thus, the available evidence indicates that even though this part of Merkes was occupied until the end of the Old Babylonian Period, it seems not to have been inhabited at the beginning of the Kassite Period. This last point, it must be emphasized, may not necessarily have been true for other parts of the city. Except in the excavations on Merkes, no Kassite or Old Babylonian occupation levels have ever been reached in excavations at Babylon.

In order to facilitate the comprehension of the discussion that follows, we will summarize the stratigraphy of the key sites involved before turning to their ceramic remains. Additional stratigraphic details will be included, as needed, in the presentation of the ceramic evidence.

2.1. PRINCIPAL STRATIGRAPHICAL SEQUENCES AND THEIR CHRONOLOGICAL ARRANGEMENT

Alluvial Plain

Tell ed-Dēr (Sippar-Amnānum)

Operation A, Phases Ie, Ic, and Ia [55] supply the basic stratigraphic framework for northern Babylonia during the Early Old Babylonian Period, that is, approximately the time of Hammurabi and Samsuiluna. A relatively secure date for the beginning of the earliest of these phases (Ie) is provided by two short-term loan contracts found in the older Phase Ig and dated to years 7 and 8 of Sîn-muballiṭ.[56]

Operation E Ensembles V-III [57] and Operation F Ensemble I [58] provide the framework for the Late Old Babylonian Period, the final century of the First Dynasty of Babylon. The latest dated text in Operation E was found in Phase IIIb, in the archive of Ur-Utu, and is dated to Ammiṣaduqa year 18 (= 17+b), month 5, day 1.[59] Operation F produced no texts.

The Kassite Period is best represented by the excavations in Operation E3.[60] The earliest Kassite context in Operation E3, Phase Ic, sits atop a complex deposit representing the abandonment of the site in the final years of the Old Babylonian Period. Phase Ia represents a subsequent Kassite occupation, while the latest, Ensemble 0, consists of pits at the modern surface, in which were found typical Late Kassite ceramics. No dated texts were found in Operation E3.

Burial 392, found at the modern surface of Operation F and cutting into the Late Old Babylonian Ensemble I, contained morphologically early Kassite vessels.[61]

---

54 REUTHER 1926, 8, fig. 7, 8 and 9, and Pl. 47-48, 52 : c.

55 *TD* 2, 67-69, 98-108, 127.

56 DE MEYER 1978, 153 : 34, Di 58 and 37, Di 60 ; for the stratigraphic location of all dated documents found in Operation A, see *TD* 2, 127.

57 GASCHE 1989b, 75-99, Pl. 25-41. For Ensemble IV, see now JANSSEN *et al.* 1994, 110-111, 122.

58 GASCHE 1989a ; PONS 1989.

59 GASCHE 1989b, 105. The last known mention of Sippar-Amnānum before the fall of Babylon comes in a text dated to Samsuditana year 6 (WATERMAN 1916, 76), some nine years later, but it is not certain whether this text mentions Sippar-Amnānum as a living city, or only as a toponym.

60 GASCHE 1991 ; MINSAER 1991.

61 PONS 1989, 22-23.

The possibilities for dating the earliest Kassite ceramics at Tell ed-Dēr in the absence of direct documentary testimony will be considered when the pottery evidence is reviewed below.

Tell ed-Deylam (Dilbat)

Second-millennium levels were uncovered in a sounding designated Area B.[62] Levels V-II have been assigned to the Late Old Babylonian Period, after the time of Samsuiluna, on the basis of their associated pottery. Level I has been assigned to the Late Kassite Period, again based on its pottery. A systematic collection of surface ceramics at ed-Deylam revealed no sherds from the time-span between the Late Old Babylonian and Late Kassite Periods. This suggests that, if the site was occupied at all, it must have been only sparsely inhabited during those decades.

Nippur

Several excavations at Nippur have provided relevant second-millennium material.

Areas TA and TB,[63] both excavated in the 1940s and 1950s, contained Old Babylonian levels. These have recently been studied and revised by E. Stone,[64] whose chronology and designations we use for the Old Babylonian levels where they differ from the original publication : Levels XIIA-XA in Area TA and Levels II-D in Area TB. The latest dated Old Babylonian tablet from good context in Area TA, dated to Samsuiluna year 29, was from Level XA.[65] In Area TB, the latest Old Babylonian tablet from good context, dated to Samsuiluna year 26, was from Level E-2.[66] Thereafter there was a gap in occupation marked by the accumulation of wind- and water-laid deposits excavated in Area TC, immediately adjacent to Area TA on the south.[67]

Area WB Level IV has produced the same Old Babylonian ceramics as the Old Babylonian contexts in Areas TA and TB. The latest text from Level IV was dated to Samsuiluna year 13.[68] Over the top of Level IV was laid a deposit of wind- and water-laid silt,[69] representing the abandonment of the area between the time of Samsuiluna and the Kassite Period.

The excavation of the earliest Kassite level in Area TA, Level VIII, and all later levels in the area was marred by a major lack of stratigraphic control. The archaeological material from these levels has had to be reassigned based on the results from more recent excavations in the adjacent Area TC [70] and on a reexamination of the original Area TA field records.[71] Thus, the results from Area TA are to some degree controlled by finds from excavations elsewhere at Nippur and from other sites, but TA's sequence still provides important information. The latest Kassite material in Area TA

---

62 ARMSTRONG 1992 summarizes the excavations at Tell ed-Deylam.

63 MCCOWN and HAINES 1967, 34-149.

64 STONE 1987.

65 STONE 1987, 118 : Table 23.

66 *Ibid.*

67 ARMSTRONG and BRANDT, 1994.

68 CIVIL 1975, 128, No. 11 and FRANKE 1978, 64.

69 FRANKE 1978, 63.

70 GIBSON 1984.

71 ARMSTRONG 1989, 99-174.

can be dated to the latter half of the thirteenth century by texts from a small business archive abandoned on the final living floor of a Late Kassite building ; the latest dated text in the archive is from Kudur-Enlil year 6.[72]

The pits and burials of Area WB Level III produced Kassite ceramics that were older in shape than the pottery of the succeeding Level II. Level III produced no dated texts. The end of Level II could be dated to the latter part of the thirteenth century based both on its pottery and on textual evidence.[73]

Area WA Level IVC, the earliest post-Old Babylonian context, consisted of pits containing Kassite shapes that are morphologically older than the pottery of Level IVB.[74] The pottery of Level IVB, the Kassite Gula Temple, can be dated to the thirteenth century based on comparisons with pottery from other contexts.[75]

In Area WC-1 [76] the end of the occupation of Level II has been placed in the latter half of the thirteenth century by a text dated to Šagarakti-Šuriaš year 4 that was found in the occupational debris above its uppermost excavated floor.[77] Levels III and IV extend back in time from the latter half of the thirteenth century.

Other excavation areas at Nippur have yielded Late Kassite shapes that can be dated to the thirteenth century based on their similarity to the pottery from dated contexts.

Middle Euphrates

Khirbet ed-Diniye (Ḫarādum) [78]

The earliest document found at this site is dated to Samsuiluna year 26, and was found in Layer 3C.[79] From this time the occupation of the town continued without significant rupture until Layer 3A, dated to Ammiṣaduqa year 18 (= 17+b),[80] a period of slightly more than a hundred years. The site was then abandoned until the eleventh century.[81]

---

72 ARMSTRONG 1989, 128-129 and 163. This archive, 2NT 740-763, was found in Locus 90 Level IV, which was dated to the early first millennium (see MCCOWN and HAINES 1967, Pl. 75 : A). The texts were not considered in the dating of the level due to non-communication between epigrapher and archaeologist. Locus 90 has been reassigned to the Kassite Period.

73 FRANKE 1978, 70. None of the dated tablets found in the excavation of WB Level II was from a stratigraphically certain context, as a result of the disturbances created by the nineteenth-century excavations in this area, However, there seems to be no doubt that the tablets were from the palace exposed in Level II. They date to the thirteenth-century reigns of Kudur-Enlil, Šagarakti-Šuriaš, and Kaštiliašu IV, so a late thirteenth-century date for the end of the level seems assured.

74 GIBSON 1978a, fig. 19 : 1 and 3.

75 The pottery from WA Level IVB, particularly from contexts inside the Gula Temple, is largely unpublished. For vessels from contemporary contexts outside the temple, see GIBSON 1975, 49, fig. 32 : 2-3 (field Nos. : 11 N 146 and 11 N 194 ; see p. 39 for proveniences), and 61-62, figs. 43-44.

76 ZETTLER 1993.

77 ZETTLER 1993, 23.

78 The site lies about 80 km southeast of Mari, on the right bank of the Euphrates.

79 There is an earlier layer, 3D, which was probably built at the time of Zimri-Līm, but it seems that the town was abandoned for a short period after the conflict between Hammurabi and Zimri-Līm (JOANNÈS 1992, 31).

80 JOANNÈS 1992, 34.

81 KEPINSKI-LECOMTE 1992, 9.

Diyala Basin

Tell Zubeidi

Tell Zubeidi lies in the Hamrin Project Area, near the Diyala River on its right bank. Thirteenth-century texts were recovered from Level I, the latest dated to the reign of Enlil-nādin-šumi (1224).[82] Artifacts found in Level I have led the excavator, R.M. Boehmer, to extend its duration into the early twelfth century.[83] Level II, undated by texts, extends back through the thirteenth century. The pottery from Level II is essentially similar to that from Level I.

Yelkhi

Yelkhi, to the northwest of Tell Zubeidi, is located near the center of the part of the Hamrin Project Area that lay north of the Diyala River. The long stratigraphic sequence at Yelkhi has been partially published in preliminary reports.[84] Most relevant to the present study are the ceramics from Levels II and I, which can be dated to the Late Kassite Period.

At this point, however, it is necessary to make a short excursus to discuss the dating of Levels IV and III, because of the presence of a type of goblet [85] that is characteristic of these levels. This shape is in several respects morphologically similar to Babylonian goblets of the Kassite Period from the Babylonian heartland (compare Fig. 1 with Pl. 1 : 23-24). Since the Babylonian goblets in question are central to our discussion of second-millennium chronology, it is imperative that we examine the relationship between them and the goblets from Levels IV and III at Yelkhi.

Above Level V at Yelkhi, dated to the Isin-Larsa Period, there is a clear stratigraphic break.[86] Levels IV and III follow, the latter having been dated by the excavators to the end of the Isin-Larsa Period and the time of Hammurabi [87] because of the presence, in the fill below III,[88] of a text (HY 224) that has been thought to bear the name of Ibâl-pī-El II, the Ešnunna king contemporary with Hammurabi. The reading of the king's name, however, is highly suspect on several grounds.[89]

---

82 BOEHMER and DÄMMER 1985, 79. All dates of Kassite reigns cited in this chapter follow those of Brinkman 1977, 337-338. We will suggest slightly lower dates in Chapter 3.

83 BOEHMER and DÄMMER 1985, 80.

84 INVERNIZZI 1980 ; BERGAMINI 1984.

85 BERGAMINI 1984, 236, fig. 57 ; and BERGAMINI *et al.* 1985, 54, 3rd col., second goblet from the top.

86 The dumping of administrative tablets on the floor of one room in the Level V palace, the presence of very large storage vessels, some still containing grain, in two other rooms along with traces of fire, and the presence of an unburied equine lying in an adjacent street all attest to the fact that this building was abandoned, apparently suddenly, and was never reoccupied (BERGAMINI 1984, 236-238). The structures of Level IV bear no relation to those of Level V, the remains of which were leveled off and filled to create a horizontal surface for Level IV (BERGAMINI 1984, 234).

87 INVERNIZZI 1980, 35-39 ; BERGAMINI 1984, 229-238 ; and BERGAMINI *et al.* 1985, 49-56.

88 Pers. comm. G. BERGAMINI.

89 In text HY 224 rev. 2', ROUAULT and SAPORETTI (1985, 26) read *ù I-ba-a*[*l-pi-El*]. According to the collation of L. De Meyer and M. Tanret (September 1997), the line in question reads either *ù i-ba-al-*⌜x⌝-[…], where the broken sign is a slanted wedge that could be part of PI, or possibly *ù i-ba-qàr-r*[*u*]. It is followed by two better preserved lines containing the penalty phrase 1 MA.NA KÙ.BABBAR Ì.LÁ.⌜E⌝ *ù li-*⌜*ša*⌝*-an-šu i-la-pa-at*, "[He] will pay one mina of silver and 'touch' his tongue" (rev. 3'-4'), which, in other contracts from the Diyala region, is always preceded by the expression *bāqir ibaqqaru*, "Whoever raises a claim …" (compare, for example, *UCPSP* 10/1 126 No. 52 : 16-18, *TIM* 5 4 : 17-19, and *TIM* 5 21 : 20-22 [these passages also use the verb *šalāpu*, "to tear out"]). There is no reason at all to have the name of Ibâl-pī-El mentioned at this particular place in the text. Where the name of the king appears in

Fig. 1. Goblet from Yelkhi (HY 123, Level IIIb. Courtesy Yelkhi Expedition). Scale : 1/6.

This fact, in addition to the tablet's discovery in secondary archaeological context — in the fill below Level III — nullifies HY 224's usefulness in helping to fix a date for that level.

The texts from Level III itself,[90] however, do suggest a lower chronological limit for Levels IV and III. In these undated texts mimation is consistently employed, which indicates that they were probably written before the time of Ammiṣaduqa, in whose reign mimation began to be used much more rarely.[91] This conclusion is premised, of course, on the assumption that the scribes at the peripheral site of Yelkhi were up-to-date with contemporary Babylonian scribal practice. Nevertheless, even allowing for the phenomenon of time-lag, these Level III tablets are still best dated to some time before the last part of the Old Babylonian Period.

Returning to the Yelkhi goblet (Fig. 1), we note that it is represented by numerous excavated examples in Levels IV and III at Yelkhi. On the other hand, goblets of this shape have never been found in any excavation west of the Tigris, that is, on the alluvial plain. Virtually identical vessels, however, have been found at the lower Diyala Valley sites of Ishchali[92] and Tell Asmar,[93] where they were attributed — 45 years ago — to the Larsa, Late Larsa and Old Babylonian Periods. This goblet, therefore, appears to be at home in the Diyala Basin. Of greatest interest to us is a published example from Level II of Tell edh-Dhiba'i, situated just east of the Tigris inside modern Baghdad.[94]

Also from Level II at Tell edh-Dhiba'i came another goblet,[95] this one belonging to the Babylonian ceramic tradition. This second goblet is very close in shape and size to our Plate 1 : 12 from a Late Old Babylonian context at Tell ed-Deylam that dates approximately to the period after

such contexts, it is always found in a declaration that an oath has been sworn, as in: MU ^{d}TIŠPAK *ù I-ba-al-pi-El* LUGAL IN. PÀ.DÈ.MEŠ, "They swore an oath by Tišpak and Ibâl-pī-El, the king," which is then followed by *ba-qir i-ba-qa-ru* ... "Whoever raises a claim ..." (compare *TIM* 5 21 : 18-20). There is far too little room on the tablet to allow both the restoration of these formulae and the retention of Rouault's and Saporetti's reading of a royal name in rev. 2'.

90 ROUAULT and SAPORETTI 1985.

91 We owe this information to L. De Meyer, who had the opportunity to examine these texts in September 1997.

92 DELOUGAZ 1952, Pl. 184 : C.547.720.

93 DELOUGAZ 1952, Pls. 121 : f and 184 : C.547.720.

94 AL-GAILANI 1965, Pl. 1 : 6.

95 AL-GAILANI 1965, Pl. 1 : 2.

Samsuiluna. The Tell edh-Dhiba'i and Tell ed-Deylam examples are small versions of the typical Late Old Babylonian goblet, which we will present below in Section 2.2.1. On the assumption that the Babylonian and Diyala goblets at Tell edh-Dhiba'i indeed came from the same level, we propose that the Diyala goblets from Yelkhi and elsewhere were being used during at least part of the Late Old Babylonian Period.

As for the other pottery from Levels IV and III at Yelkhi, we have concluded that in the Old Babylonian Period the Diyala Basin, including the Hamrin, has to be considered peripheral to the Babylonian heartland. Even though it had a distinguishable pottery-making tradition, it nevertheless shared general characteristics. Thus, among the open forms from these levels several have good parallels in the Old Babylonian material from the Northern Alluvial Plain. Additionally, a nearly whole small bottle with black-painted decoration [96] and several sherds from similar vessels were found in Level IV.[97] These bottles are diagnostic for the period of Hammurabi and Samsuiluna in Babylonia proper, and they indicate that Level IV cannot be earlier than the time of Hammurabi, and could well be later.

Taken together, the foregoing data suggest that Levels IV and III at Yelkhi can be dated broadly to the Old Babylonian Period. As for the distinctive goblet characteristic of these levels (Fig. 1), we have no evidence to indicate how much longer after the end of Level III it continued to be made. Nevertheless, we do know that while this shape was produced east of the Tigris, it was not at home in the Babylonian heartland ; and we know that on present evidence it can be securely associated only with contexts that are significantly earlier than those of the Babylonian goblets it most closely resembles (Pl. 1 : 23-24).

A second stratigraphic break — longer than that between Levels V and IV — separates Levels III and II at Yelkhi. Based on their pottery, Levels II and I are contemporary with Tell Zubeidi Levels II and I and thirteenth-century levels at sites in Babylonia proper.

Susiana

Susa

Operation A of the Ville Royale at Susa, excavated by R. Ghirshman,[98] provides crucial data for our argument because its stratigraphic sequence does not show any significant break between the Old and Middle Elamite Periods.[99] In other words, there was continuity in occupation at Susa during the period of widespread deurbanization in southern Mesopotamia before and after the fall of

96 BERGAMINI 1984, 236, fig. 64, where this vessel, according to Bergamini (pers. comm.), is incorrectly attributed to Level V.

97 Pers. comm. G. Bergamini. An additional black-painted sherd was found in an unsure context attributed to Level Va.

98 The second-millennium pottery sequence from the Ville Royale excavations was published by GASCHE 1973. STEVE *et al.* 1980 present an updated survey of the archaeological and epigraphic evidence from the second-millennium levels of the Ville Royale.

99 The Susa material has been worked and reworked over the last several decades. It is not our intention to go over old ground again, so, where necessary, we will refer to the latest studies, without tracing in detail the path to the conclusions held at present. The stratigraphic table recently published by DESCHESNES (1996, 37), which gives a questionable temporal distribution of the levels excavated by Ghirshman in Operations A and B of the Ville Royale, should be disregarded.

Babylon.[100] Because much has been written about the second-millennium levels of the Ville Royale and because some of the information used here for dating has been published only recently, we will present the archaeological and documentary evidence from Susa in more detail than has been the case for the other sites.

The Ville Royale levels of primary significance here are, from lowest to highest, A XIII, A XII, and A XI. The differences between the chronology presented here and that found in the earlier presentations of the Ville Royale sequence [101] arise primarily from our use of the sequence of sukkalmahs published by F. Vallat [102] and from the subsequent identification of the name of Kuk-Našur III on seal impressions from Level A XII.[103] This new information has resulted in new synchronistic relationships between Levels A XIII and A XII of the Ville Royale and the chronology of the First Dynasty of Babylon.

Level A XIII: The documents that help establish the date for the end of A XIII were found in two locations. First, from the debris of Locus 66, a room in one of the smaller A XIII houses, which was built during the latter part of the level,[104] came a house-sale contract that included an oath in the name of Tan-Uli, sukkalmah (written sukkal.GAL).[105] According to Vallat's new sequence, Tan-Uli is the second known sukkalmah after the reign of Kuk-Našur II.[106] This Kuk-Našur, in turn, is mentioned in a text from Dilbat dated to year 1 of Ammiṣaduqa.[107]

The second piece of evidence comes from a cache of 139 tablets that we now know was buried under Locus 120, an A XIII street.[108] The latest identifiable texts in this cache are four letters from the sukkal of Susa, Temti-halki,[109] who later succeeded Tan-Uli as sukkalmah.[110] The house-sale contract mentioning Tan-Uli and the group of letters of Temti-halki are, therefore, contemporary with one another. Because of the synchronism between Kuk-Našur II and Ammiṣaduqa, these documents

---

100 In the absence of physical methods for dating, the absolute dating of all Elamite dynasties depends entirely on several direct or indirect synchronisms with Babylonian rulers. All absolute dates for second-millennium contexts in Susiana are ultimately based on the same sources as in Babylonia.

101 Principally GASCHE 1973 and STEVE *et al.* 1980.

102 VALLAT (1994) is based upon the more thorough presentation found in VALLAT (1990), as corrected in VALLAT (1993). See also VALLAT (1996b) for more details on this issue.

GLASSNER (1996) has also recently proposed a sequence for the sukkalmahs from Šilḫaḫa to the Kuk-Našur contemporaneous with Ammiṣaduqa. We find this sequence to be unconvincing because it is in total contradiction with the archaeological *realia*. The practical effect of Glassner's proposal is to turn the relevant stratigraphy of Susa upside down. For a review of Glassner's article from the standpoint of the textual evidence, see VALLAT 1997b.

103 STEVE 1994, 26-27.

104 For the location of Locus 66, see STEVE *et al.* 1980, fig. 4. Field records show that this house, constructed on top of the ruins of the "Complexe Central" of Level A XIV, was built later than the Level A XIII houses located on the northern side of the excavation area.

105 STEVE *et al.* 1980, 89 and 128 *sub* TS.XIII.20.

106 VALLAT 1994, 13.

107 UNGNAD 1909, 3 ; see also SCHEIL 1932, 150, No. 24 for additional information about this text.

108 See STEVE *et al.* 1980, 89, for a discussion of the findspot of this tablet cache.

109 Referred to as "maire de Suse" (= sukkal of Susa) by De Meyer in STEVE *et al.* 1980, 89.

On 17 published legal texts, also found at Susa, the name of Temti-halki is invoked in oath formulae after that of Tan-Uli (SCHEIL 1930, 7 : 36, 9 rev. 7, 20 : 11, and 113 rev. 7 ; 1932, 171 rev. 5, 173 rev. 18, 177 rev. 3, 186 : 2, and 247 : 17 ; 1933, 335 : 10, 336 : 9 and rev. 10, 337 rev. 6, 338 : 7, 339 : 3, 353 : 42, 369 rev. 19 ; and 1939, 416 : 29). This sequence shows clearly that when Temti-halki was sukkal of Susa, as is mentioned in the four letters from Level A XIII, Tan-Uli must have been sukkalmah (see also DE MEYER 1982).

110 Temti-halki, sukkalmah, appears on several bricks found at Susa (SCHEIL 1900, 77, Pl. 15 : 1-4 ; 1905, 27, Pl. 6 : 4).

must be more-or-less contemporary with the last years of the First Dynasty of Babylon. Therefore, we propose that the end of Level A XIII should be dated to approximately the same time as the fall of Babylon. It cannot be significantly earlier.

Level A XII: There is no significant break between Levels A XIII and A XII. Level A XII buildings, including the large "Complexe Est," were mostly rebuilt along the same general lines as before. The continuity in the material culture of the two levels can be seen in their pottery as well.

Some of the architectural remains in Level A XII can be assigned to earlier and later phases within the level ; we will refer to these phases as Lower Level A XII and Upper Level A XII.

During Level A XII, Susa passed into the period contemporary with the little-known decades after the fall of Babylon. From Locus 6 along the western edge of the excavation area, from an Upper Level A XII floor, came a legal text bearing an impression of the seal of Kidinū, "king of Susa and Anzan." [111] At some point before the end of Level A XII, therefore, this king replaced the last of the sukkalmahs — on present evidence Kuk-Našur III.[112]

Traces of this dynastic change may survive in the remains of Level A XII. In the eastern part of the level, excavators uncovered the above-mentioned "Complexe Est." [113] In Lower Level A XII this large building was the residence of Attaru-uktuh,[114] a person of some importance in Susa, who had been corresponding with the sukkalmah. At least a portion of Attaru-uktuh's archives were found in this building.[115] Fifty-five tablets were lying on the floor in front of the door,[116] indicating that the house had been abandoned in haste, and that the owner had never been able to return to recover the documents left behind. From this building came several letters from an unnamed sukkalmah. One of them bears the seal of the last known sukkalmah, Kuk-Našur III, as does the fragment of an envelope.[117] We suggest, then, that the abandonment of these archives and the residence in which they were stored is connected with the downfall of the last sukkalmah. The end of Upper Level A XII, as we have already seen, postdates the beginning of Kidinuid rule. Attaru-uktuh's residence was not reoccupied in Upper Level A XII.

The documentary evidence from Levels A XIII and A XII provides us with a close chronological sequence. First, the latest texts from Level A XIII are all contemporary with Tan-Uli, second known successor to Kuk-Našur II, the contemporary of Ammiṣaduqa. Then, from Lower

---

111 Kidinū revived, in modified form, an old style of Elamite titulature that had not been used for more than four hundred years, since the reign of the first sukkalmah, Ebarat (STEVE *et al.* 1980, 92-94).

112 VALLAT 1994, 13. [x]-matlat, whose name comes after Kuk-Našur III in Vallat's table of rulers, is attested once on a tablet (TS IX : 91) bearing the seal of Kuk-Našur III (STEVE 1994, 26-27), where he has the title "king (lugal) of Susa" (STEVE *et al.* 1980, 90). Therefore he must have been a contemporary of Kuk-Našur III.

QUINTANA (1996) has suggested that there are at least four different Kuk-Našurs in the sequence of sukkalmahs. Independent of any assessment of the correctness of his reconstruction, we note that his Kuk-Našur IV is the same as the ruler here identified as Kuk-Našur III (see also VALLAT 1997c).

113 For the location of the "Complexe Est," see STEVE 1994, fig. 2.

114 This Attaru-uktuh should not be confused with the Attar-uktuh mentioned in the later so-called "Malamir Texts" (STEVE *et al.* 1980, 126).

115 Loci 115-116 (= one room during Lower Level A XII, but divided by deep foundations from Lower Level A XI) and locus 160 (see STEVE *et al.* 1980, 126-127, fig. 16). Other tablets were found in Locus 153.

116 Loci 115-116.

117 TS XII : 91 and 91bis from Locus 153 (STEVE 1994, 26-27).

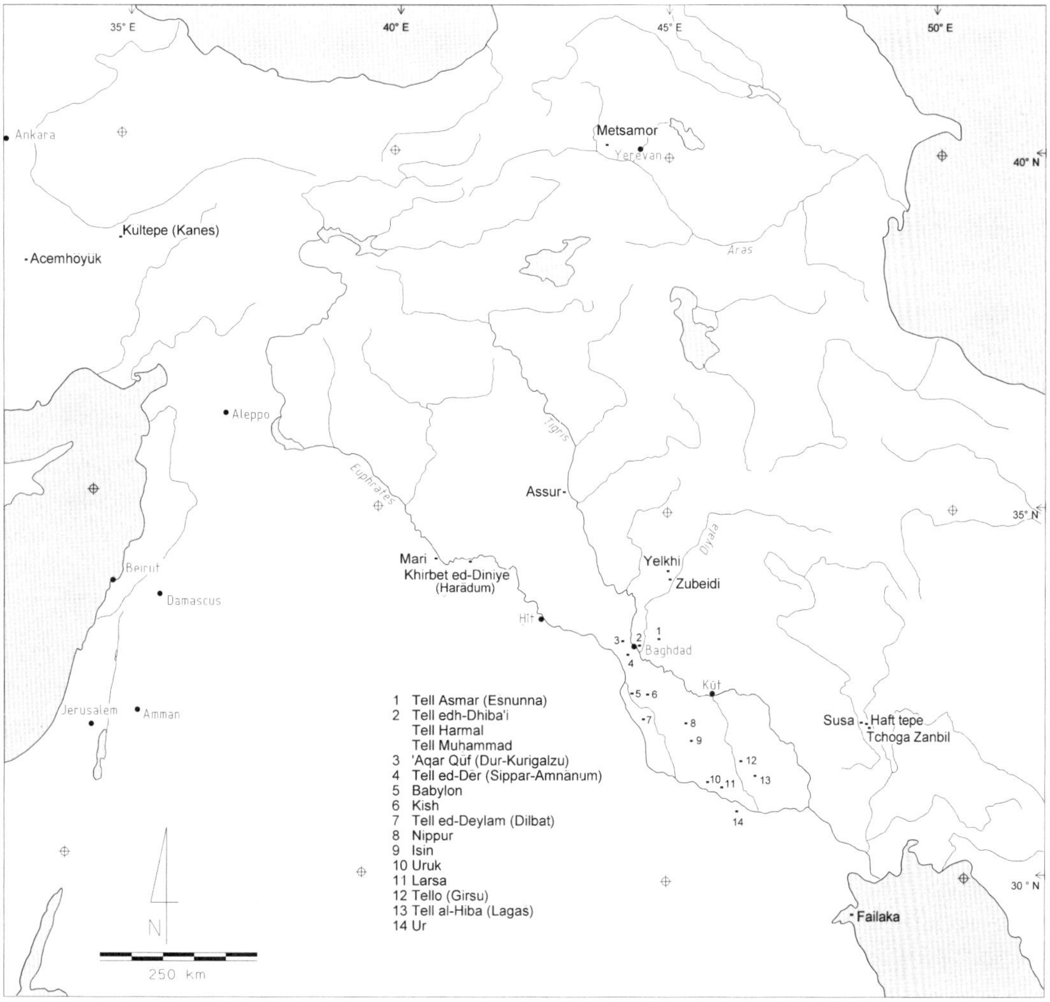

Fig. 2. Map Showing the Sites Mentioned in the Text.

Level A XII, we have seal impressions and at least one letter from Kuk-Našur III, the second known ruler after Tan-Uli and the last known sukkalmah. Finally, from Upper Level A XII comes a seal impression of Kidinū, who ruled as "king of Susa and Anzan" in the period after Kuk-Našur III.[118]

Although the upper end of this sequence can be tied reasonably closely to Babylonian chronology, the lower end is chronologically less secure. We do not know the exact dates or length of Kidinū's reign. The fifteenth-century dates attributed to the period of the Kidinuids in general are

[118] The sequence in which Kidinū and the other four Kidinuids ruled cannot be determined from the available evidence. Kidinū was the son of ^{d}IM.SAR.GAL (= ^{d}*Adad-šarru-rabû*?), who is not known to have been a king (STEVE *et al.* 1980, 92; and Amiet in STEVE *et al.* 1980, 139). The filiations of the others are unknown. Steve's reconstruction of the sequence, which places Kidinū first, appears to be the most plausible, based on paleographic evidence (STEVE *et al.* 1980, 92-98). However, our chronological arguments are not dependent on the exact sequence for this group of rulers.

derived from an early-fourteenth-century synchronism between Pahir-iššan, the second ruler of the following dynasty of the Igihalkids, and Kurigalzu I of Babylonia.[119]

Therefore, the documentary evidence cannot be adduced to support a close date for the end of Level A XII, either in absolute terms or in terms of Babylonian chronology. We would suggest a time-span of about five decades for the level as a whole. In earlier publications time-spans of 150 years [120] and 120 years [121] were proposed for this level. These estimates have always seemed to be unreasonably long, and arose, not from the archaeological evidence itself, but from the *a priori* adoption of the Middle Chronology for the dating of the sukkalmah levels at Susa.

Level A XI : Any interpretation of the finds of Level A XI is complicated by the failure on the part of the excavators to recognize that the level, as dug, consisted of two distinct phases (at least in the western half of the excavation), and to separate the finds accordingly. The earlier phase, Lower Level A XI, is comprised of architectural remains that in part, at least, represent a rebuilding of structures from A XII (STEVE 1994, Fig. 1). There is, however, a perceptible decline in the quality of construction and the durability of structures. Above these remains was a deposit consisting of numerous thin layers of debris without any traces of architecture. Thus, there is a break between Lower Level A XI and the Level A X above.[122] We can now say, however, that after a reexamination of the stratigraphy and the published pottery, there is a demonstrable continuity between A XII and Lower Level A XI, which is evidenced not only by the architecture, but also by their respective pottery assemblages.[123]

In addition, an abandoned archive, found in a house from Lower Level A XI,[124] contained documents mentioning several of the later sukkalmahs,[125] who were contemporary with Levels A XIII and Lower A XII. On these grounds as well, then, Lower Level A XI cannot be far removed in time from the levels immediately beneath.

It has been proposed that Susa declined during the period of the Kidinuids, at a time when the nearby settlement of Haft Tepe was the recipient of royal beneficence.[126] On the contrary, we stress that Upper Level A XII and Lower Level A XI must date to the time of the Kidinuids. Thereafter,

---

119 VAN DIJK 1986 ; STEVE and VALLAT 1989. The previous thirteenth-century date for Untaš-Napiriša, proposed first by CAMERON (1936, table III) and largely followed thereafter, is based on a questionable restoration by SCHEIL 1908, 85, l. 3 (text : [x-x-*l*]*i-ia-aš*), cf. Reiner *apud* ROWTON 1976, 218. Even if the reliability of the material in a literary text like the "Berlin Letter" (VAN DIJK 1986) is open to debate, it should be noted that the synchronism between Untaš-Napiriša and Burna-Buriaš II (1359-1333) indicated in this document better fits the ceramic evidence from Tchoga Zanbil than does the thirteenth-century date suggested by Cameron.

120 GASCHE 1973, plan 10 and STEVE *et al.* 1980, 78.

121 STEVE 1994, 28.

122 STEVE *et al.* 1980, 123 *sub* TS.XII.1-12.

123 GASCHE 1973, 15 and plan 7 (groups 1, 9, 11), and plan 8 (groups 19 to 22). This particular point will be developed in a future reexamination of the pottery of the levels in question.

124 Loci 024, 027 and 028, contiguous to the "Complex Est" of Lower Level A XI (see STEVE 1994, 29, fig. 1), built above the house of Attaru-uktuh in Lower Level A XII.

125 STEVE 1994, 25-26.

126 Among many others, see CARTER 1970, 201 ; PORADA 1975, 368 ; and AMIET 1988, 85.

More generally, it can be observed that despite the emphasis in recent years on the purported building activity of Tepti-ahar at Haft Tepe, all known building inscriptions of this king have been found at Susa ; none have been found at Haft Tepe thus far.

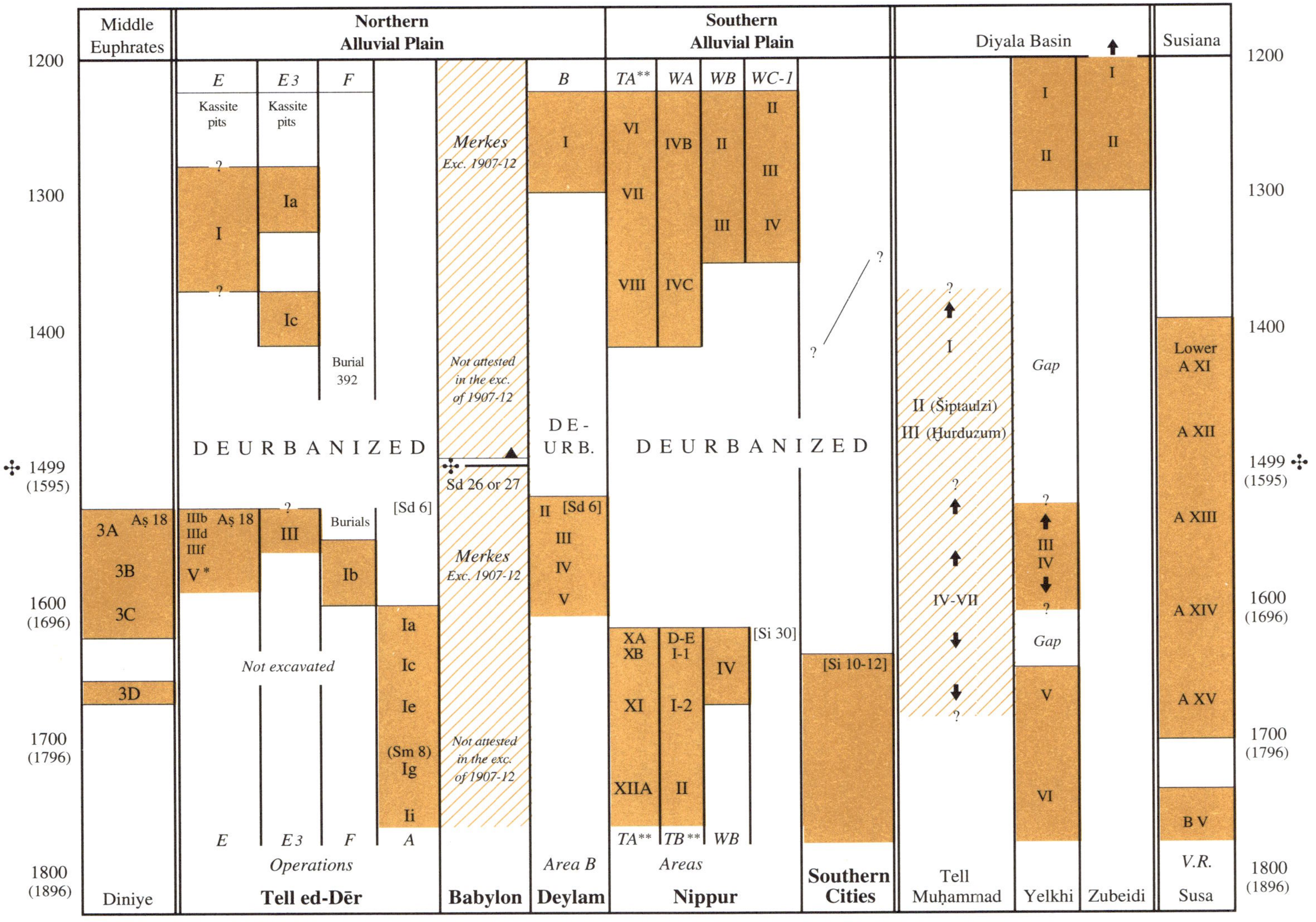

Fig. 3. Comparative Stratigraphy of Key Second-Millennium Sites.

(1595)	Middle Chronology dates.
Aş 18	Ammiṣaduqa, year 18 = date of the latest OB text found in regular excavations.
[Sd 6]/[Si 30]	Samsuditana, year 6/Samsuiluna, year 30 = date of the latest known OB text from the site(s).
(Sm 8)	Sîn-muballiṭ, year 8 = latest dated text found in a stratigraphic unit.
V.R.	Susa, Ville Royale, Operations A and B.
✣	Fall of Babylon (1499 BC, see Chapter 5).
▲	Suggested date for the resettlement of Babylon (1496 BC, see Chapter 5).
*	For Ensemble IV, see now JANSSEN *et al.* 1994, 110-111, 122.
**	For Area TA Levels VI-VIII, see ARMSTRONG 1989, 99-174 ; for TA Levels XIIA-XA and TB Levels II-D, see STONE 1987.

however, there was a serious rupture in the stratigraphical record of Operation A, represented by the accumulation above Lower Level A XI. The area was reoccupied only after a lapse of two centuries or more.

As was the case with Level A XII, the duration of Lower Level A XI can only be estimated. However, we will not be far from the truth if we suggest a time-span on the order of fifty or sixty years.

2.2. The Pottery Sequence

Our purpose in this section is to identify and describe vessels that can be attributed to the Early Kassite Period, that is, the period extending from the time of the fall of the Old Babylonian Kingdom to the well-attested Late Kassite Period of the thirteenth century. Then, utilizing the available archaeological evidence, we will propose dates for these Early Kassite vessels and, by extension, for their archaeological contexts, without making prior assumptions about the chronology of the First Dynasty of Babylon.

In our presentation of the pottery sequence we focus on three groups of closed shapes : goblets, jars, and cups (Pls. 1-3).[127] What is most important about these vessels, in contrast with the rest of the corpus, is that there are sufficient data about each of them to trace their morphological and technological evolution through the middle centuries of the second millennium. Of the three, the goblet is the most informative, because it is the most frequently and widely attested shape in the whole of the second-millennium Babylonian ceramic corpus, having been produced by the tens of thousands. Goblets were apparently essential to every second-millennium Babylonian household ; they were continually being broken and in need of replacement. The mass production of the goblet necessitated by this continuous demand meant that its shape became increasingly standardized over a wide area. This standardized shape, because it was complex, was prone to change, and, in fact, it evolved continually over the course of the centuries. Mass production ensured that the evolution of the goblet's shape remained uniform across a relatively broad region. The ubiquitous second-millennium goblet, therefore, provides a very sensitive indicator of the passage of time within the Babylonian heartland and for this reason receives the bulk of our attention.[128]

In contrast with the closed forms, the principal open forms — bowls and platters — are much less useful. Platters, even though they are very diagnostic in Old Babylonian times, had entirely ceased being manufactured by the end of the Old Babylonian Period. Only a few bowl forms survived the transition to the Kassite Period, and although they were produced in large quantities, their geometrically simple shapes changed little during the period under examination here. Old Babylonian and Kassite bowls can be distinguished, but within the Kassite Period chronological

---

127 These terms are used here simply for convenience of reference.

128 We emphasize the point that a stratigraphically anchored sequence of mass-produced ceramic forms provides a very strong relative chronological framework and frequently offers a more objective basis for dating than, for example, real estate documents (which, although dated, can remain in archives for a long time), cylinder seals (which can continue to be used for generations after their manufacture), and statues, reliefs, or even figurines (all of which can remain inside a building for much longer than a common pot).

distinctions cannot be made. Larger forms also changed shape too slowly to be diagnostically useful, and they have not been excavated and/or published in sufficient numbers. Other distinctive forms and decorative characteristics are diagnostic for only short periods.

We first discuss the better-dated Old Babylonian and Late Kassite assemblages before turning to the poorly defined and virtually unknown Early Kassite material that the former bracket in time.

2.2.1. Pottery Assemblages from the Old Babylonian and Late Kassite Periods

The Early Old Babylonian Period (Approximately the Time of Hammurabi and Samsuiluna) [129]

Goblets (Pl. 1). The goblets from northern (Pl. 1 : 14-17) and southern (Pl. 1 : 25-28) Babylonia in the Early Old Babylonian Period share morphological characteristics, though their shapes are sufficiently different that they would not be mistaken for each other. In both regions they are characterized by a bottom-heavy, almost baggy, appearance and have no shoulder to speak of. However, examples from the South tend to have a less well defined neck than contemporary examples from the North. In the South the rims simply curve out from upper bodies that are more-or-less vertical or only slightly sinuous. In the North, on the other hand, the goblets tend to have a neck that is set off from the upper body by a constriction, to which may be added a slight horizontal incision (Pl. 1 : 16-17).

The bases of second-millennium goblets were made in several different ways ; the differences that have been observed have both geographical and temporal significance.

Babylonian potters developed techniques for dealing with the tendency of bases to crack during the drying process prior to firing. It should be noted that much of what follows applies not only to the bases of goblets, but to the bases of other forms, open and closed, as well.[130]

A. Van As and L. Jacobs have identified and described the three solutions of second-millennium Babylonian potters to the problem of cracked bases.[131] Clay that had been tempered with coarse vegetal matter figured in each of these solutions, because such clay strengthened the bases and made them less likely to crack during drying. The potter could utilize one of these three methods to strengthen the base : 1) repair the cracks after they appeared with coarsely tempered clay ; 2) deliberately leave a hole in the vessel's bottom that would then be filled with a plug of coarsely tempered clay (Fig. 4) ; or 3) add coarsely tempered clay to a hole in the center of the cone of clay on the wheel, so that as the vessels were thrown, their bases for the most part came to be filled in with

---

129 We have used period names and definitions that are meaningful for the archaeological material we discuss. Our usage does not necessarily conform to that of, for example, epigraphers or historians.

130 For the present these techniques are attested only from the beginning of the second millennium, but nothing excludes the possibility that they were being utilized earlier. Until now, however, ceramics from the third millennium have not been systematically examined.

131 VAN AS and JACOBS 1987. See also MINSAER 1991, 46.
Most of the detailed information presented here having to do with manufacturing techniques is based on observations made on the pottery excavated at Tell ed-Dēr and, to a lesser extent, at Susa. Having looked at the pottery from most of the sites included in our larger study of the second-millennium Babylonian ceramic tradition, A. Van As and L. Jacobs observe that in general the same manufacturing techniques characteristic at Tell ed-Dēr were used in all locations (VAN AS and JACOBS 1988, 1-3 and A. Van As, pers. comm.).

the coarser material,[132] a method that Van As and Jacobs have called "preventative strengthening" (Fig. 5).[133] For brevity's sake we refer to bases that were made according to Method 2 as "plugged," and those made according to Method 3 as "filled-in."

When a cross-section of a base is examined, the strengthening technique, if any, utilized by the potter can be seen. Plugged bases are attested from both northern and southern Babylonia during the Early Old Babylonian Period (Pl. 1 : 15 and 26). Evidence for filled-in bases at this period is ambiguous. If the coarsely tempered clay in the base of the goblet in Plate 1 : 25 does not represent the repair of cracks by Method 1, then it may be the earliest attested example of a filled-in base.[134] Otherwise, on present evidence, the filled-in base is not attested until the Late Old Babylonian Period.[135]

The method of strengthening a base, if any, and the shape of a base are not the same thing. Bases of greatly differing sizes and shapes could be made following the same technique, while bases of the same shape might be made in different ways.[136]

The bases of the goblets fall broadly into two shape categories : 1) bases that range from being essentially flat to consisting of a short, often twisted, stump (Pl. 1: 14 and 17) ; and 2) bases consisting of a pedestal or ring-like foot (Pl. 1 : 15-16 and 25-28). The variation in shape found among the first group of bases seems to be due largely to the cursory manner in which the potter finished the base. These bases usually show traces of the string that was used to separate them from the wheel. It must be noted, however, that some stump bases were plugged, at least by Late Old Babylonian times.[137] Bases belonging to the second group were made by drawing out and shaping the clay at the bottom of the vessel into a ring (Pl. 1 : 9-10, 15-16, and 25-28) or, especially in Late Old Babylonian times, a small, low pedestal (Pl. 1 : 11-13).

Within Babylonia, goblets with the flat or stump bases of the first group have been found only in the northern area. Those belonging to the second group, with drawn-out and shaped bases, are attested in both the North and the South.

At Susa, on Babylonia's southeastern periphery, goblets with the flat or stump bases of the first group appear in Level A XV of the Ville Royale. These goblets are virtually identical to those

---

132 As the walls of such a vessel were raised, part of the more coarsely tempered clay was sometimes drawn up as well and coated the lower part of the vessel's interior (see Pl. 1 : 6).

133 VAN AS and JACOBS 1987, 47.

134 The goblets illustrated in Plate 1 : 25 and 26, from older excavations at Larsa and Tello respectively, were examined and drawn in the Louvre. Their chronological position in Plate 1 is based on the fact that they cannot be later than Samsuiluna year 10, the date by which the southernmost Babylonian cities were abandoned (GASCHE 1989b, 128-129 and Plan 8).

135 Data on how bases were manufactured have not yet been collected in a systematic manner for the Early and Late Old Babylonian Periods at Tell ed-Dēr. We are not sure if the apparent relative rarity of the filled-in base among those vessels that have been examined has any significance. We cannot state which method, if any, was most commonly used. On the other hand, data have been systematically collected for Kassite ceramics, and the potters' preference for the filled-in bases produced by Method 3 is demonstrable (VAN AS and JACOBS 1988, 2).

136 For example, compare the bases of PONS 1989, Pl. 6 : 6-9. The base of No. 7 is plugged. No. 9 has a filled-in base. No. 8's may be filled in as well, although it may have been repaired according to Method 1. No. 6 shows no indication that any of the three techniques for strengthening was used in its manufacture. The shapes of all four bases, nevertheless, are almost the same.

137 GASCHE 1989b, Pl. 32 : 2. The fact that plugged stump bases are not attested earlier may be due to the fact that at the time the relevant levels were being excavated at Tell ed-Dēr, this information on manufacturing techniques was not being systematically collected.

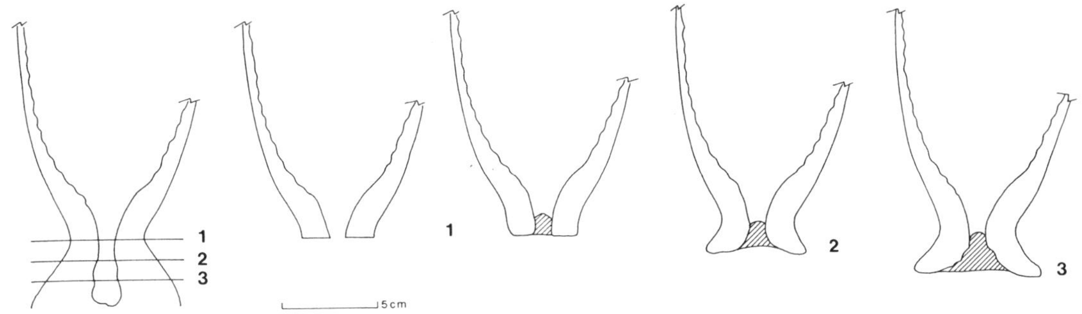

Fig. 4. Strengthening the Base by Method 2 (Plugged Base) ; after VAN AS and JACOBS 1987, Fig. 3.

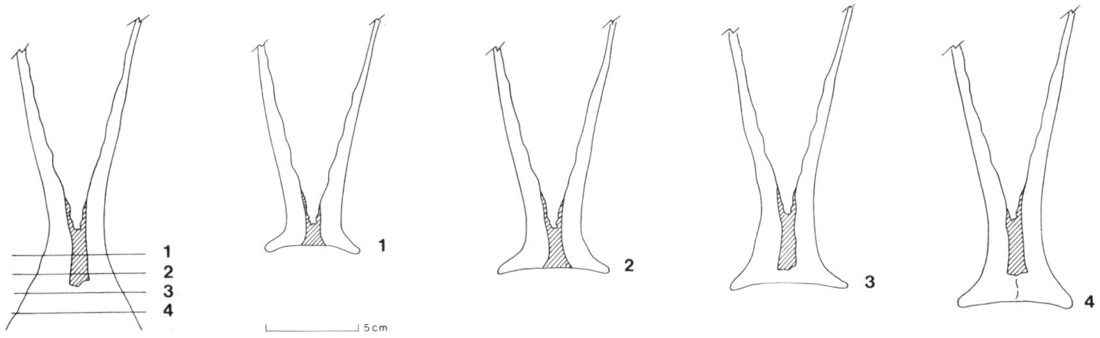

Fig. 5. Strengthening the Base by Method 3 (Filled-in Base) ; after VAN AS and JACOBS 1987, Fig. 4.

found in northern Babylonia (Pl. 1 : 37 ; compare Pl. 1 : 17). The presence of these goblets in Levels A XV and A XIV (Pl. 1 : 36-37) helps date these levels to a time contemporary with the Early Old Babylonian Period in the absence of dated or datable texts. These goblets were incorporated into the ceramic assemblage of Susiana relatively soon after their introduction, and they began to follow an indigenous developmental path and became an important component in the local assemblage. The profiles of later Susiana goblets from Level A XIII and Lower Level A XII (Pl. 1 : 34-35) diverge substantially from those of contemporary Babylonian examples (Pl. 1 : 9-13).

Jars (Pl. 2). The jars from Tell ed-Dēr in northern Babylonia are well-made vessels characterized by a cylindrical neck of medium height with a simple tapered rim,[138] a globular or spherical body with its maximum diameter at the midpoint of the body, and a true ring base (Pl. 2 : 9). Jars of this description are almost exclusively found in northern Babylonia. Based on the evidence from Tell ed-Dēr,[139] they appeared first during the reign of Samsuiluna. In southern

[138] The rims of these jars in some cases are thickened and have been beveled or beaded.

[139] GASCHE 1989b, 88-89.

Babylonia the typical small-to-medium sized jar of the Early Old Babylonian Period had a short vertical-to-everted neck that was frequently decorated with black paint.[140]

Cups (Pl. 3). Cups with medium-to-tall necks are found exclusively in northern Babylonia in this period ; no examples have been found in the South. The earliest known examples from Phase Ic of Operation A at Tell ed-Dēr (Pl. 3 : 8-10) have spherical bodies and cylindrical or slightly everted necks of medium height with simple, tapered rims. Cups are attested in both plain and fine wares. The plain-ware examples have thicker vessel walls and flat or stump bases (Pl. 3 : 9), while those in fine ware have thin walls and delicately made ring bases (Pl. 3 : 8 and 10). This shape was still relatively rare in the Early Old Babylonian Period, but became more common thereafter.

During the Early Old Babylonian Period, related but distinguishable ceramic traditions [141] existed in northern and southern Babylonia. However, the distinct southern ceramic tradition disappeared from the archaeological record as a result of the deurbanization of the South that began early in the reign of Samsuiluna. Shapes that could be successors to those in use in the South during the reign of Samsuiluna have not yet been identified at Nippur or at any site to the south of it. Based on present evidence, therefore, after about Samsuiluna year 30, the continuing development of Babylonian ceramics involved only those shapes that belonged to the northern tradition. The vessels that were later manufactured and used in southern Babylonia during the Kassite Period evolved not from the southern ceramics of the Early Old Babylonian Period, but from the Late Old Babylonian shapes of northern Babylonia, to which we now turn.

The Late Old Babylonian Period (Approximately the Time from Abi-ešuḫ to Samsuditana)

Tell ed-Dēr, where the post-Samsuiluna ceramic corpus was first identified and described,[142] has the most complete assemblage from the Northern Alluvial Plain for the last century of the Old Babylonian kingdom.[143] Most of our information for the ceramics of this period comes from the excavations at this site.

Goblets (Pl. 1). The northern goblets from the century after the collapse of the South show morphological differences from their earlier counterparts. These goblets generally have their maximum diameters somewhat higher than before, near the midpoint of the body, and have begun to lose the bottom-heavy appearance they had in the previous century (Pl. 1 : 9-13). Smaller examples sometimes occur (Pl. 1 : 12). Alongside plugged bases (Pl. 1 : 10), filled-in bases (Pl. 1 : 9) are also present. Bases in the Late Old Babylonian Period frequently have the shape of small, low pedestals (Pl. 1 : 11-13).

---

140 E.g., FRANKE 1978, fig. 60 : 3 ; and VAN ESS 1988, fig. 14 : 108.
A rare, if not unique, example of a northern jar found in the South was excavated in a burial at Isin (KARSTENS 1981, 44 [Grab 62]) and Pl. 35 : IB 850). Even though this jar contained a tablet dated to Hammurabi year 39 (WALKER and WILCKE 1981, 95, IB 899), the burial was cut from a level in which the latest texts were dated to Samsuiluna year 26.

141 "Ceramic tradition" here refers to the customs and manufacturing techniques that lie behind — and are revealed in — the shapes and technical features of vessels produced in large quantities by professional potters.

142 GASCHE 1989b, 75-99.

143 An essentially similar ceramic assemblage has been excavated in Area B at Tell ed-Deylam (ancient Dilbat), but without dated texts (ARMSTRONG 1992).

Goblets belonging to the Babylonian tradition are also present at Khirbet ed-Diniye (Ḫarādum) on the Middle Euphrates (Pl. 1 : 1-3). The Diniye goblets have their maximum diameters at the midpoint of the body or slightly higher; some have plugged bases (Pl. 1 : 2). Several examples from Diniye have higher maximum diameters than are found on contemporary goblets from northern Babylonia (Pl. 1 : 1). The Diniye examples look almost Kassite in shape, and in this respect they anticipate the subsequent development of goblets in the Babylonian heartland.

Jars (Pl. 2). The Late Old Babylonian globular jars from Tell ed-Dēr show little change in shape from the time of Samsuiluna (Pl. 2 : 7-8), and they continue to be well made, with true ring bases. In general, the examples from Diniye are somewhat smaller than those in northern Babylonia (Pl. 2 : 1-2). An unusual plugged jar base is attested from Diniye (Pl. 2 : 1).

Cups (Pl. 3). In the post-Samsuiluna period, medium-to-tall-necked cups occur more frequently at Tell ed-Dēr than they had previously, and they show definite morphological changes from before (Pl. 3 : 5-7). Most noticeably the neck is taller in relation to the body, and, as a result, the vessels lose their earlier squat appearance and become more graceful. The bodies themselves remain essentially spherical with their maximum diameters at their midpoints. These cups continue to be attested in both plain (Pl. 3 : 5) and fine (Pl. 3 : 6-7) wares. The fine-ware examples have walls that are very thin and display a consistent gracefulness of form and delicacy of manufacture that is unparalleled among other Old Babylonian vessels.

The Late Kassite Period (13th-Early 12th Centuries)

In general, the Late Kassite ceramic corpus, characterized by a limited number of different forms and by a seeming lack of care in its manufacture, is fairly well known. It can be placed chronologically with certainty at least from the early thirteenth century down into the twelfth.

Datable thirteenth-century Late Kassite levels have been excavated in several areas at Nippur, including Area WC-1 Level II [144] and Area WB Level II.[145] In both areas the latest dated Kassite texts are from the latter half of the century. Other Late Kassite contexts at Nippur have been identified and attributed to the thirteenth century by comparing their pottery with the better dated assemblages from these areas. In Area WC-1, Levels IV and III, without dated texts, extend back through the thirteenth century and into the fourteenth.

Toward the end of the thirteenth century, most of Nippur was abandoned,[146] and no early twelfth-century contexts have been identified at the site.

Other thirteenth-century contexts have been excavated in the Hamrin, part of the Diyala Basin, on the northeastern periphery of Babylonia. Tell Zubeidi Level I produced thirteenth-century texts, the latest coming from the reign of Enlil-nādin-šumi,[147] and thus a late thirteenth-century date for the ceramics of Tell Zubeidi Level I is clear. Based on twelfth-century comparisons for other artifacts

---

144 ARMSTRONG 1993, 74.
145 FRANKE 1978, 66-70 ; see also ARMSTRONG 1993, 73-74.
146 ARMSTRONG 1989, 208-219 ; see also BRINKMAN 1984, 175.
147 BOEHMER and DÄMMER 1985, 79.

from Level I, the excavator, R.M. Boehmer, has extended its duration into the first half of the twelfth century.[148]

The excavations carried out at the Kassite city of Dūr-Kurigalzu (ʿAqar Qūf) during the Second World War should have provided important data to help work out the ceramic chronology of the Kassite Period, but the pottery from the site was never adequately published. A single photograph shows examples of the pottery from the four levels of the palace at Tell al-ʾAbyaḍ, one of the mounds of which the site is constituted.[149]

The vessels identified in the photo as being from Level I of Tell al-ʾAbyaḍ look the same as pottery from known thirteenth-century contexts. According to the excavator, the pottery from Level IA, the latest phase of Level I, consisted of "standard Kassite types which are not distinguishable from those found in the earlier strata."[150] Level I is closely bracketed chronologically by the latest dated tablets from Level II (Kaštiliašu IV [1232-1225])[151] and from the palace's final destruction in Level IA (Marduk-apla-iddina [1171-1159]).[152] Therefore, the evidence from ʿAqar Qūf allows us to draw, at the very least, the conclusion that typical late thirteenth-century pottery forms continued in use into the twelfth century.

The inadequate publication of the pottery, when combined with uncertainties about the chronology of the earlier levels of the Tell al-ʾAbyaḍ palace, severely limits ʿAqar Qūf's usefulness in establishing the chronology of the earlier stages of Kassite ceramic development. Nevertheless, an observation by the excavator bears repeating, because it is consistent with what has been found to be true at other sites : "the workmanship of the pots tends to be less crude as we descend from Level II to the foundation level (Level IV)."[153] That is to say, the earlier Kassite pottery tends to be better made than the later.

Two recently excavated northern Babylonian sites, Tell ed-Dēr[154] and Tell ed-Deylam,[155] as well as Tell Yelkhi in the Hamrin Project Area,[156] have also produced Late Kassite pottery. In the absence of dated texts, this material has been broadly attributed to the thirteenth century based on comparisons with better-dated collections from Nippur and the Hamrin.

Goblets (Pl. 1). Late Kassite goblets are characterized by high, well-defined shoulders and slender bodies that taper in an almost straight line to a small drawn-out base (Pl. 1 : 4-5, 18-20, and 29-30). Like all Late Kassite ceramics, they are frequently carelessly made, and tend to be irregularly shaped. Indeed their very irregularity can almost be considered a diagnostic characteristic. These goblets occur in a fairly broad range of sizes, between about 24 and 36 cm in height, wherever they have been found. In Plate 1, it can be seen that the smaller (Nos. 4, 20, and 30) and larger (Nos. 5, 18-19, and 29) examples display the same overall slender proportions.

---

148 BOEHMER and DÄMMER 1985, 80.
149 TAHA BAQIR 1945, Fig. 25.
150 TAHA BAQIR 1945, 9.
151 *Ibid.*, 10 and 12-13.
152 *Ibid.*, 9 and 12.
153 *Ibid.*, 14.
154 Ensemble 0, see GASCHE 1991 and MINSAER 1991.
155 Area B Level I, see ARMSTRONG 1992, 221-222.
156 Levels II-Ia, see INVERNIZZI 1980, 31-34 ; BERGAMINI 1984, 224-229 ; and BERGAMINI *et al.* 1985, 54 top and 56.

The flat or stump base of Old Babylonian times never occurs on these vessels. Likewise, the plugged base has not been attested. The goblets that have been examined have filled-in bases that tend to be thick, forming a solid foot that is usually at least two or three cm high and sometimes more than ten cm.

The slimmer, straighter profile of the goblet's lower body in the thirteenth century and the increasing frequency of the solid foot are related phenomena. As the body of the goblet became narrower and more tapered, the potter, because he could no longer reach the inside bottom of the vessel with his hand, had a more difficult time trying to estimate the correct height at which to separate the newly thrown vessel from the clay cone in order to produce a base of ideal thickness.[157] The thickness of such a base would have resulted in cracking during drying. However, Late Kassite potters utilized the preventative-strengthening technique, our method 3, which produced filled-in bases. The use of this technique meant that potters could produce goblets in great numbers very quickly, while still being able to minimize the almost unavoidable tendency of their thick bases to crack.[158] Thus thick bases — solid feet — came to be typical in the Late Kassite Period. The weight of their bases also lowered the center of gravity of these tall, potentially top-heavy vessels.

Jars (Pl. 2). The Late Kassite jar tends to be considerably smaller than its Old Babylonian forerunner and lacks the earlier vessel's spherical shape (Pl. 2 : 3, 10, and 13). Instead, the maximum diameter is above the midpoint of the body, resulting in a more-or-less well-defined shoulder. In the shaping of this shoulder, there is a distinction between the jars of northern Babylonia and the contemporary shapes from the South. The northern jars, from sites like Tell ed-Dēr and Tell ed-Deylam in Babylonia, tend to have almost a carination that sets the upper body or shoulder off from the lower body (Pl. 2: 3). Jars from the South tend to have more rounded profiles and, consequently, less well-defined shoulders (Pl. 2 : 10). Not surprisingly, the jars from the Ḥamrin Basin frequently have the more carinated profile common in northern Babylonia (Pl. 2 : 13). The typical base everywhere is the drawn-out, filled-in base, made in the same way as in the Late Kassite goblets.

Cups (Pl. 3). The Late Kassite cups differ markedly from the cups of the Late Old Babylonian Period (Pl. 3 : 1-2, 11-12, and 15). The fine-ware shapes are no longer being produced ; all examples are in plain ware and are frequently rather carelessly made. There are two groups of cups, differentiated by a clear difference in size : examples can be classed as either small (Pl. 3 : 1, 11) or large (Pl. 3 : 2, 12). In other respects both groups of cups are essentially similar. They have tall necks with concave profiles, and their bodies typically have an inverted piriform shape that tapers from a wide shoulder to a small pedestal base. The base was manufactured in the same way as the bases of the Late Kassite goblet and jar. Though it is a less common shape than the goblet or jar, the Late Kassite cup is highly diagnostic, being found all across northern and southern Babylonia and in the Diyala Basin as well.

---

157 VAN AS and JACOBS 1987, 41 and 49-50.
158 VAN AS and JACOBS 1987, 47-49.

2.2.2. The Early Kassite Period

In the previous section we have identified the pottery of the final phase of urban occupation in southern Babylonia, from the time of Samsuiluna ; we have carried the corresponding sequence from northern Babylonia forward an additional century, to a point late in the reign of Ammiṣaduqa, at which time well-documented evidence from the alluvium ceases ; and we have established that the well-known shapes of the Late Kassite assemblage were being produced in the thirteenth and early twelfth centuries. From this survey it can be seen that the Old Babylonian and Late Kassite forms, particularly in the case of the goblets, are substantially different from one another. The Early Kassite material to which we now turn substantially fills the developmental gap between the earlier and later vessel shapes.

Early Kassite Contexts

Contexts with Early Kassite ceramics have been identified at only two Babylonian sites, Tell ed-Dēr and Nippur.

At Tell ed-Dēr this pottery has been found in Operations F and E3. In Operation F, Burial 392 — uncovered at the heavily eroded modern surface — was cut down into Late Old Babylonian occupational remains (Phase Ib) that have been dated to the time of Abi-ešuḫ and Ammiditana.[159] In Operation E3 the earliest post-Old Babylonian occupational remains, Phase Ic, sit atop a complex deposit that accumulated during the years immediately before and after the end of the Old Babylonian Period. Phase Ia follows Phase Ic after an occupational gap indicated by the general lack of architectural continuity between the two phases and by the differences between their respective pottery assemblages. Phases Ia and Ic are cut by several large pits (Ensemble 0) containing typical Late Kassite pottery.

At Nippur, Early Kassite contexts have been identified in several areas. Level IVC of Area WA consisted of ash-filled pits that were cut down into the ruins of the Old Babylonian Gula Temple (Level V). These pits were sealed by the Kassite Gula Temple of Level IVB, from which came typical Late Kassite ceramics. Area WB Level III consisted largely of pits and burials that were cut down into Level IV, a house that had been abandoned during the reign of Samsuiluna. Level III was covered by the walls and pavements of the Level II palace, from which came Late Kassite pottery. Finally there is Area TA Level VIII, the earliest Kassite level in Area TA,[160] which was excavated, as has been demonstrated, with insufficient stratigraphic control.[161] From this level, however, comes a vessel that we have included in our presentation because of its morphologically early shape, despite the problems with its excavated context.

---

159 GASCHE 1989a, 22-23.
The only remains of the latest Late Old Babylonian occupation in Operation F — approximately contemporary with Operation E Phases IIId-IIIb — were eight Late Old Babylonian burials that had been cut down into Phase Ib (GASCHE 1989a, 21-22 ; and p. 25 above). The living floors of that occupation were completely eroded away.

160 McCOWN and HAINES 1967, 68.

161 ARMSTRONG 1989, 99-176.

Relative Chronology

By comparing the ceramic assemblages from these contexts with one another and with the Late Old Babylonian and the Late Kassite assemblages, we can arrange the vessels and their contexts in relative chronological order.

From a morphological standpoint the two vessels from Burial 392 in Operation F at Tell ed-Dēr are the earliest of our Early Kassite forms from Babylonia. In several respects the goblet (Pl. 1 : 8) is intermediate in shape between the Late Old Babylonian and later goblets. Its maximum diameter is just above the midpoint of the body, and its shoulder is not as well defined as it would subsequently become. At the same time the body is wider and rounder than it tends to be in later goblets. In shape, the neck is poised between the everted necks typical of Late Old Babylonian times and the vertical, concave necks typical of Late Kassite. It has a filled-in base, also a characteristic of the Late Kassite Period.

The jar from Burial 392 (Pl. 2 : 6) is likewise distinguishable from the Late Old Babylonian jars. The body is not spherical, as it would have been in the Late Old Babylonian Period, and its maximum diameter has shifted to just above the midpoint of the body. Nevertheless, it still lacks a well-defined shoulder and its body is rounder than would be the case later on. It has a shaped, filled-in base, in contrast to the true ring bases typical of the Old Babylonian jars. Thus both the jar and goblet have the "earliest-looking" profiles among our Early Kassite vessels, profiles that are not very far removed from those of the Late Old Babylonian Period.

No complete goblet profiles were found in Tell ed-Dēr Operation E3 Phase Ic. While the goblets from Phase Ic (Pl. 1 : 6-7) have the broad profile of the goblet from Burial 392, nevertheless, their lower bodies are less rounded and appear to have higher and, as a result, somewhat better-defined shoulders (Pl. 1 : 7). Around 90% of the goblets that have been examined from Phase Ic have filled-in bases (Pl. 1 : 6), a characteristic they share with virtually all later Kassite goblets.[162] However, the occasional use of the plugged-base technique, found frequently on Old Babylonian ceramics, is still attested in Phase Ic (Pl. 1 : 7).

The marked concavity of the neck and the slight shaping of the shoulder of a jar from Phase Ic Burial 374, (Pl. 2 : 5) give it a later appearance than the jar from Burial 392 (Pl. 2 : 6). These differences, together with the differences between the goblets, lead us to place Operation E3 Phase Ic somewhat later than Operation F Burial 392. The jar in Plate 2 : 5 has a filled-in base, but plugged bases are also attested on jars from Phase Ic.

A cup from Operation E3 Phase Ic (Pl. 3 : 4) has a body that is still almost spherical, but a slight tapering of the lower body serves to distinguish it from the rounder shape of Late Old Babylonian cups. Even though this cup, like most later Kassite examples, is made in plain ware, its shape nevertheless has something of the gracefulness of the Late Old Babylonian fine-ware cups. This is the earliest cup thus far attested to have a filled-in base as opposed to a ring or stump base.

The goblets from Nippur Area WA Level IVC (Pl. 1 : 23-24) had been deposited secondarily in large ash-filled rubbish pits that also contained many fragmentary Middle Babylonian exercise

---

162 See also VAN AS and JACOBS 1988, 1-2.

tablets.[163] These are the earliest-looking goblets that have been identified at Nippur.[164] In comparison with the goblet from Tell ed-Dēr Operation F Burial 392 (Pl. 1 : 8), they appear to be somewhat later : their shoulders are better defined and their lower bodies are more tapered. Their necks are fully vertical and concave. However, their shapes and proportions are still substantially different from those of typical Late Kassite goblets. They remain significantly shorter, broader and rounder than their later counterparts.

A jar from Nippur Area TA Level VIII (Pl. 2 : 12) is virtually identical with the jar shown from Tell ed-Dēr Operation E3 Phase Ic (Pl. 2 : 5). Even though its excavated context is problematic, it is important to identify the presence of this morphologically early shape at Nippur. Based on their shapes, this jar and the goblets from the pits of Level IVC mentioned above represent the earliest Kassite vessels thus far identified at Nippur.[165]

In terms of shape, the goblets from Nippur Area WB Level III, two of which are illustrated in Plate 1 (Nos. 21-22), fall between the Early Kassite goblets we have already seen and those of the Late Kassite assemblage. These goblets are close to those of the thirteenth century in their overall proportions, and their shoulders are more pronounced than any from Early Kassite Period that we have hitherto described.[166] They consistently lack the solid foot that is commonly found in Late Kassite examples. Moreover, they are well shaped and well finished, characteristics that they share with the other Early Kassite vessels we have already seen [167] and that distinguish them in general from the thirteenth-century vessels.

The occupational deposits from the palace in Area WB Level II, which covers Level III, do not allow us to trace with any precision the transition of the forms characteristic of Level III into the typical Late Kassite goblets.[168]

This transition is apparent, however, in the goblets from the excavations at Area WC-1. We have already mentioned the Late Kassite material from Area WC-1 Level II, which can be assigned to the latter half of the thirteenth century. Beneath Level II, Level III and a small portion of the upper part of Level IV were also excavated.

---

163 GIBSON 1978a, 12-13 ; CIVIL 1978, 12 N 577-580, 582-599, and 651-655.

164 WOOLLEY and MALLOWAN 1976, Pl. 108 : 77 show a vessel from Ur that, within the limitations of its very schematic rendering, looks similar to the goblets of Area WA Level IVC and Tell ed-Dēr Operation E3 Phase Ic. However, it is only about two-thirds the size of the Nippur examples. Moreover, it was associated with Old Babylonian vessels, including a typical southern goblet from the Early Old Babylonian Period (see Pl. 107 : 69c), in an intramural burial (Burial LG 161) from House 30/C [see p. 168]).

165 We have not been able to identify other Early Kassite shapes from Area TA Level VIII. Most vessels from this level were not drawn, but were only categorized according to the field typology. It is possible that some Early Kassite shapes were grouped together with their corresponding Late Kassite shapes, which, having been encountered first in the excavation, were used to establish the field typology.

166 Goblets shorter than the ones illustrated also come from Area WB Level III. Examples are shown in GIBSON 1978b, 118, fig. 15, where the tallest goblet, on the left, is our Plate 1 : 21.

167 GIBSON 1978b, 118 ; MINSAER 1991, 43 ; and TAHA BAQIR 1945, 14.

168 There was no significant buildup of occupational debris on the original floor of the palace (Level IIC). This floor was covered with 30 cm of fill, which underlay an upper floor (Level IIB), on which was found material from the time of the building's abandonment in the late thirteenth century (FRANKE 1978, 66-70).

The goblet bases from Area WC-1 Level IV and from the early floors of Level III all have interiors that are open to the bottom of the vessel.[169] None has a solid foot.[170] Even though only the lower part of the body has been preserved in each case, it appears that the goblets represented by these bases resemble the goblets from Area WB Level III. In the later floors of Area WC-1 Level III slimmer, lower bodies and solid feet begin to supplant the earlier form.[171] In the stratigraphy of Area WC-1, then, the transition to the typical Late Kassite form is apparent.

Returning to Area WB, we find that the jars from Level III (Pl. 2 : 11) are also intermediate in shape between the jars from Nippur Area TA Level VIII (Pl. 2 : 12) and Tell ed-Dēr Operation E3 Phase Ic (Pl. 2 : 5) on the one hand, and the smaller Late Kassite examples (Pl. 2 : 3, 10, and 13) on the other. The jar from Tell ed-Dēr Operation E3 Phase Ia (Pl. 2 : 4) is very close in shape to the Level III jars of Area WB.

The cups from Area WB Level III include examples (e.g., Pl. 3 : 13) that are very similar to the cup from Tell ed-Dēr Operation E3 Phase Ic (Pl. 3 : 4). Alongside these, however, are cups whose bodies are substantially less spherical (Pl. 3 : 14). They are not yet Late Kassite in shape, however (compare Pl. 3 : 1, 11, and 15). Further distinguishing them from the Late Kassite cups is the fact that they are very well shaped and finished. Finally, in Level III the cups are all more-or-less of one size ; the larger and smaller variants of the thirteenth century were not yet being produced.

Tell ed-Dēr Operation E3 Phase Ia is the latest of the pre-Late Kassite contexts, based on the character of its pottery. Phase Ia has yielded goblets that resemble those from the other Early Kassite contexts ;[172] however, goblets with Late Kassite shapes come from here as well, including one very similar in shape to Plate 1 : 4.[173]

The jar from Phase Ia does not have a thirteenth-century shape (Pl. 2 : 4). Morphologically it stands in an intermediate position between the Early (Pl. 2 : 5) and Late (Pl. 2 : 3) Kassite jar shapes from Tell ed-Dēr and, as we have already noted, most closely resembles the examples from Nippur Area WB Level III (Pl. 2 : 11). Plate 2 : 4 has a plugged base, but filled-in bases are equally attested from this context.

As was true with the goblets, Phase Ia yielded cups with both Early[174] and Late Kassite (Pl. 3 : 3) shapes. By the time of Phase Ia, therefore, goblets and cups seem to have assumed their Late Kassite forms. However, the Phase Ia pottery assemblage as a whole is not yet fully Late Kassite in character ; that stage is not reached in Operation E3 until the succeeding Ensemble 0 with the pottery from the pits.[175] Taken together, the stratigraphical and morphological data suggest that

---

169 ARMSTRONG 1993, 75 and Pl. 79 : a-i.

170 When solid-footed Kassite goblets were disposed of in antiquity, their bases remained as cylinders or cones of baked clay that were virtually indestructible. If solid-footed Kassite goblets had been in use in the early contexts of Area WC-1, traces of them would have readily become incorporated into the archaeological record. The absence of these bases is therefore significant.

171 ARMSTRONG 1993, Pl. 79 : j-dd.

172 See, for example, MINSAER 1991, Pl. 10 : 2, 6, 8.

173 MINSAER 1991, Pl. 10 : 10.

174 *Ibid.*, Pl. 12 : 1-2.

175 *Ibid.*, Pls. 9, 11, 13, 15, 17 and 19 : 4-15.

Phase Ia is best placed chronologically between Nippur WB Level III and the full-blown Late Kassite of the thirteenth century.

The Early Kassite contexts from Babylonia have been arranged chronologically as follows: Tell ed-Dēr Operation F Burial 392 is the oldest, based on the shapes of the vessels from the burial. Tell ed-Dēr Operation E3 Phase Ic and Nippur Area WA Level IVC come next, along with the jar from Nippur Area TA Level VIII (Pl. 2 : 12). Nippur Area WB Level III is next, followed by Tell ed-Dēr Operation E3 Phase Ia, which immediately precedes contexts exhibiting the fully developed Late Kassite assemblage.

With the Early Kassite material from Tell ed-Dēr and Nippur we have largely filled the developmental gap between the Late Old Babylonian and the Late Kassite pottery assemblages. That the gap has almost been eliminated can be seen by comparing Plate 1 : 8 (Early Kassite) to Plate 1 : 1 and 11 (Late Old Babylonian). It is therefore now possible to trace the gradual transition in vessel shapes from the Early Old Babylonian Period to the beginning of the twelfth century, and to see, for example, that the bottom-heavy Early Old Babylonian goblets and the slender, high-shouldered Late Kassite goblets are indeed connected to one another in a discernible evolutionary continuum.

The Evidence from Susa

The limited amount of information at our disposal pertaining to the Early Kassite Period in Babylonia proper can be supplemented and augmented by data from Susa, a site on the Babylonian periphery. We begin our examination of Susa by looking back to the era contemporary with the Early Old Babylonian Period. At that time northern Babylonian goblets with flat or stump bases were introduced into Susa in Level A XV of the Ville Royale. These goblets became a part of the local ceramic tradition and continued to be produced until Lower Level A XII (Pl. 1 : 34-37). In Upper Level A XII, a new and substantially different goblet shape appeared for the first time (Pl. 1 : 33).[176] The earlier goblets are not attested after Lower Level A XII, while the new goblets continued into Level A XI (Pl. 1 : 31-32).

When the latest of the older goblets at Susa (Pl. 1 : 34) is compared with the earliest of the newer goblets (Pl. 1 : 33), it is evident that there is not simply an incremental change in shape-evolution. The newer goblet was not an indigenous development within the local Susa ceramic tradition, but was the result of a different developmental trajectory, one in which the potters of Susa played no part before Upper Level A XII. The new goblets, it is clear, came from Babylonia. They shared the short, broad, round shape we have already seen in Tell ed-Dēr Operation F Burial 392 (Pl. 1 : 8), Operation E3 Phase Ic (Pl. 1 : 7), and Nippur Area WA Level IVC (Pl. 1 : 23-24).

That the new goblets in Upper Level A XII were introduced from Babylonia is corroborated by the fact that their bases were made utilizing a Babylonian technique that was unknown at Susa before Upper Level A XII. The bases of the new goblets were plugged in the same manner as the bases of Babylonian goblets of the Old Babylonian Period. Plugged bases first appeared at Susa in Upper

[176] Ten whole and fragmentary examples were recorded from Upper Level A XII (STEVE *et al.* 1980, fig. 5, Groupe 19, variante c).

Level A XII ; thereafter they are attested frequently. In Susiana, the successors to the goblets of Upper Level A XII always have plugged bases.[177] The filled-in base has never been observed in second-millennium contexts there.

In Babylonia, on the other hand, plugged bases became increasingly rare as the Kassite Period progressed. Even though plugged bases were present on vessels at Tell ed-Dēr in Operation E3 Phase Ic (Pl. 1 : 7) and in the succeeding Phase Ia (Pl. 2 : 4 [jar]), they were already exceptional, especially for goblets. By the time of Phase Ic, filled-in bases were typical ; they remained so throughout the rest of the Kassite Period in Babylonia.[178]

Taken altogether, the foregoing data lead us to conclude that an Early Kassite plugged-base goblet most likely entered Susa before the filled-in bases became normative for goblets in Babylonia, that is, before the time of Phase Ic in Tell ed-Dēr Operation E3. Once in Susa, this Early Kassite goblet, like the Old Babylonian goblet before it, became incorporated into the local pottery tradition fairly quickly and ceased to be truly Babylonian. The subsequent developmental path followed by the Babylonian goblet during the Kassite Period seems not to have affected the goblet in Susiana and vice-versa. Soon after the Early Kassite goblet came into Susiana, the goblets of the two regions began to look different from one another. Already in Lower Level A XI of the Ville Royale the goblets were beginning to show a non-Babylonian character (Pl. 1 : 32), the start of a separate developmental course that was not paralleled in the Babylonian heartland.[179]

As we proposed in Section 2.1, around the beginning of Lower Level A XII, Susa passed into the period after the collapse of the first Dynasty of Babylon. That conclusion is consistent with our proposal here that Early Kassite goblets, which appeared first in Upper Level A XII, came into Susa before the time of Phase Ic in Operation E3 at Tell ed-Dēr. On the strength of the evidence from Susa, therefore, we believe that there was a further development of the Babylonian goblet, as yet unattested in Babylonia proper, when the newly emerging Early Kassite shape was being produced by potters who still utilized typical Old Babylonian manufacturing techniques. Although the goblet made its way to Susa at this time, the Diyala region, on the traditional route between Babylonia and Susa, appears not to have been affected by its movement, a circumstance that either points to the existence of a road that ran south of the Diyala Basin along the Tigris and then turned eastward from the river in the direction of the piedmont, or to the use of an old, nearly forgotten, river route that had been largely bypassed in the previous centuries, going back to the Ur III Period.[180]

2.3. DATING

Unfortunately, with the exception of Level A XII of the Ville Royale at Susa, none of the contexts that are at the center of this study provides internal evidence for close dating. The dates we

---

177 Even what appears to be a goblet of the older type from Lower Level A XI was provided with a plugged base (GASCHE 1973, Pl. 19 : 6).

178 VAN AS and JACOBS 1988, 1-2.

179 Although we cannot trace the subsequent evolution of the Susiana goblets in this study, we note that over time their necks grew very tall in relation to the height of their bodies, and that the bodies themselves became slim. Examples that illustrate these developments can be seen in GASCHE 1973, Pl. 19.

180 See, for example, LEEMANS 1960, 175.

propose are approximations. Nevertheless, they are more than just guesswork. Even though only a limited amount of archaeological material is available from the Early Kassite Period, the evidence is substantial for the periods immediately before and after. In well-excavated stratigraphic sequences where the ceramics have been well recorded we have been able to track the gradual changes in vessel shapes over time during these earlier and later periods. Such changes are especially apparent in mass-produced vessels with complex shapes. Our observations of the ceramics from these better attested periods have helped inform our assessments of the chronological significance of changes in vessel shapes during the Early Kassite Period.

2.3.1. Chronology of the Early Kassite Pottery

Late Kassite pottery shapes had fully emerged by the middle of the thirteenth century in Babylonia. Therefore, we place the latest of our Early Kassite contexts, Operation E3 Phase Ia at Tell ed-Dēr, around the turn from the fourteenth to the thirteenth centuries. Area WB Level III at Nippur can then be situated slightly earlier, in the middle decades of the fourteenth century ;[181] the evolution of goblet bases through the sequence of floors and levels in Nippur Area WC-1, presented above, leads to the same general conclusion concerning the chronological position of Level III in Area WB.

We have placed Area WA Level IVC — the Nippur context with the morphologically earliest Kassite goblets — around the end of the fifteenth century and the beginning of the fourteenth. We attribute the morphologically early jar found in Area TA Level VIII to the same chronological horizon. For the dates of these vessels and contexts, we believe that the written sources offer some corroboration. Except for a very incomplete Early Kassite inscription of uncertain chronological significance,[182] the earliest documentary evidence known to be from Nippur consists of three items : a legal text dated to the reign of Kadašman-Ḫarbe I,[183] another dated to the reign of either Kadašman-Ḫarbe I or Kadašman-Enlil I,[184] and an economic text from the reign of Kurigalzu I.[185] These documents suggest that by the end of the fifteenth century Nippur had been resettled. In this way they provide some support for our contention that the earliest Kassite vessels at Nippur date to the same period.

We have attributed to Tell ed-Dēr Operation E3 Phase Ic the same late fifteenth/early fourteenth-century date as the foregoing material from Nippur, because of the morphological similarities among the vessels from the two sites.[186]

The two vessels from Operation F Burial 392 at Tell ed-Dēr (Pls. 1 : 7 and 2 : 6) are, from the standpoint of their shapes, the earliest Kassite forms thus far identified on the alluvial plain. We have dated them somewhat earlier than the material from Operation E3 Phase Ic on morphological

---

181 FRANKE (1978, 55, Table 2) originally dated the Level III material to the fourteenth century and earlier.

182 SASSMANNSHAUSEN 1994 ; see also n. 29 above for additional comments about this inscription.

183 BRINKMAN 1976, 146, K^{a}.2.1 ; 388, Text 18.

184 BRINKMAN 1976, 146, 144, J.5.5 ; 391, Text 23.

185 BRINKMAN 1976, 146, 239-240, Q.2.115.168, and p. 402, published later by DONBAZ 1987, D. 85.

186 A date around 1400 or slightly earlier for Phase Ic has already been proposed by MINSAER (1991, 47) and GASCHE (1991, 30-31).

grounds, assigning Burial 392 to the latter half of the fifteenth century.[187] Burial 392, however, has no close stratigraphical relationships, so its dating can only be very approximate. Questions about the nature of the abandonment and resettlement of Tell ed-Dēr arise when we attempt to deal with Burial 392. Even though the Late Old Babylonian city was abandoned during the last decades of the First Dynasty of Babylon, it is possible that the Temple of Annunītum remained in use; the temple's location, however, has not yet been identified. Burial 392 might have been associated with this hypothetical post-Old Babylonian occupation of the temple.[188] However Burial 392 is regarded, Operation E3 Phase Ic, on present evidence, seems to indicate the general reoccupation of Tell ed-Dēr in Kassite times.

2.3.2. Spatial vs. Temporal Variation

A comparison of the shapes of the goblets from Susa with those of the alluvium raises the issue of spatial variation (that is, regional ceramic traditions) vs. temporal variation, and how they can be distinguished.

In the present instance it can be seen that the Susa goblets (Pl. 1 : 31-33) tend to have higher necks than are found on the fifteenth-century goblets from Babylonia (Pl. 1 : 8 and 23-24). They also tend to have more pronounced shoulders. Shoulders as pronounced as those from the southeastern periphery first appear in the alluvial plain only in the middle of the fourteenth century (Nippur Area WB Level III ; Pl. 1 : 21-22), though in the arrangement of shapes shown on Plate 1 the slimmer, more tapered bodies of the mid-fourteenth-century Babylonian shapes serve to distinguish them from their earlier, stouter eastern counterparts.

Is it possible to arrange all the Babylonian and peripheral goblets in a single chronological sequence according to the shape of their shoulders ? It turns out that such an arrangement cannot be accomplished without doing violence to secure chronological and stratigraphical relationships. We have concluded that, even though shoulder shape is a chronological indicator for goblets from the Babylonian heartland (that is, the shoulders grew more pronounced over time), it is a geographical indicator within the Early Kassite Period, where less-pronounced shoulders are found in Babylonia and more-pronounced shoulders in Susiana.[189]

2.3.3. Chronology at Susa and the Date of the Fall of Babylon

In Section 2.1 we proposed a duration of Level A XII (Lower and Upper Phases together) of the Ville Royale of around five decades, substantially shorter than the 120 to 150 years imposed by the *a priori* adoption of the Middle Chronology for the dating of the sukkalmah levels at Susa. Level A XII and Lower Level A XI together represent a span of a century or so, beginning around the

---

187 Burial 392 was attributed to the fifteenth century at the time it was excavated, based on the early character of its pottery (PONS 1989, 23 ; GASCHE 1989a, 16).

188 GASCHE 1989a, 16.

189 It is tempting to see a connection between these goblets from Susa, with their pronounced shoulders, and the high-shouldered goblets from Yelkhi discussed above in Section 2.1. However, we have not yet been able to establish any connection between the two shapes in the lower Diyala Valley, where we would expect to find it.

time of the fall of Babylon.[190] A number of Early Kassite goblets and a seal impression bearing the name and titulature of Kidinū were found in Upper Level A XII, in contexts that should be dated several decades after the beginning of Lower Level A XII, therefore sometime relatively soon after the fall of Babylon.

The sequence of sukkalmahs cannot, given the present state of our knowledge, be used as proof in any chronological argument involving the archaeology of Susa, because we do not know if the reconstructed list of rulers is complete, and we do not know how long each held the throne. Nevertheless, we are still able to say that the sequence, as it is presently understood, is consistent with our shortening of the duration of Level A XII. The next-to-last known sukkalmah, Temti-halki, was attested in Level A XIII as sukkal of Susa, the postition he held during his predecessor's tenure as sukkalmah. In Level A XII there is adequate time for the end of the rule of the sukkalmahs and the beginning of the rule of the Kidinuids. It follows that Lower Level A XI, in part or in whole, should be attributed to the time of the Kidinuids, who ruled an unknown number of years extending back from around 1400.[191]

As we have already indicated, the appearance of the Early Kassite goblets in Upper Level A XII should be dated several decades after the end of Level A XIII. Because of their essential similarity to the goblets from Tell ed-Dēr Operation E3 Phase Ic and Nippur Area WB Level IVC, we place them in the fifteenth century as well. We position them somewhat earlier, around the middle of that century, because their plugged bases suggest that they came into Susiana before filled-in bases became the norm in Babylonia, i.e., by the time of Tell ed-Dēr Operation E3 Phase Ic. If the beginning of Lower Level A XII and, by extension, the end of the overthrow of the First Dynasty of Babylon [192] are only a matter of decades earlier, then the dates of both should be placed in the vicinity of 1500.

2.4. CONCLUSION

While we do not regard this dating of the fall of Babylon to around 1500 as definitive, we nonetheless believe that it is highly likely. It falls a century short of the corresponding Middle Chronology date, and more than a century and a half short of the date according to the High Chronology, because we cannot justifiably stretch out the available archaeological materials to fill the additional time mandated by those systems.

Another way to examine the issue of the quality of fit between the Middle (or High) Chronology and the available archaeological evidence is to pose the question : how long did it take for the Babylonian goblet to evolve from its shape in the latter part of the reign of Ammiṣaduqa (Pl. 1 : 11) to its shape at the end of the fifteenth century (Pl. 1 : 7 and 23-24) ? According to the Middle Chronology, the Late Old Babylonian and the late fifteenth-century shapes should be separated by two centuries.

---

190 The contemporaneity of the beginning of Lower Level A XII with the fall of Babylon is discussed above in Section 2.1.

191 For the synchronism between Pahir-iššan and Kurigalzu I that gives rise to this date, see VAN DIJK 1986 ; STEVE and VALLAT 1989 ; and Section 2.1 above.

192 Discussed above in Section 2.1.

The earliest attested post-Old Babylonian goblets at Susa, from Upper Level A XII of the Ville Royale (Pl. 1 : 33) can also be compared with the Babylonian goblets attributed to the end of the fifteenth century (Pl. 1 : 7 and 23-24). They are very close to one another in appearance, sharing the same stout proportions. We have dated the Susa goblets up to a half century earlier than the earliest Early Kassite examples from the alluvium. The Middle Chronology would increase that temporal separation to around 150 years.[193]

We believe that the duration of these intervals, as dictated by the Middle Chronology, are unreasonably long, because the pace of the shape-evolution of the vessels we have examined, especially the goblets, would be retarded tremendously in comparison with what happened before and after. It might be suggested that such a slowing in the changes of these vessels' shapes should be expected during the unsettled conditions that were attendant on the collapse of the Old Babylonian state. However, the pace of a vessel's evolution is a function of the complexity of its shape, not of the stability of its social environment. Complex shapes, which are relatively difficult for the potter to produce, will of necessity change fairly rapidly, at least from the archaeologist's standpoint. We believe that the minor degree of difference between the Late Old Babylonian and the Early Kassite shapes that we have examined are not consistent with a separation in time of two centuries or more.

Equally significant is the high degree of uniformity apparent in the morphological development of the Early Kassite vessels that we have investigated. Is that uniformity consistent with a pottery-making tradition that is fragmented and has broken down or one that is unified and continuous ? The answer to this question will help us understand the situation in the years immediately after the fall of Babylon.

The picture we derive from the archaeological and epigraphic evidence is of urban abandonment in northwestern Babylonia in the years immediately preceding the Hittite *coup de grâce*.[194] The paucity of Late Old Babylonian and Early Kassite remains from excavations leads us to conclude that many of the old urban centers were only minimally inhabited, at least in the period shortly before and after the final collapse. However, settled life must have continued at some level, though it is clear that it was not very robust. As for the capital, Babylon, evidence of Early Kassite occupation was not recovered on the mound of Merkes, the one excavation area where sufficient depth was reached.[195] One must assume that surviving traces of the Early Kassite settlement are closer to the unexcavated center of the Old Babylonian city, to which those inhabitants who remained probably would have retreated during the interval of instability.

Certainly the pottery industry would not have been immune to the consequences of this breakdown. We infer that, as the urban centers of northern Babylonia decreased in size, the level of pottery production shrank accordingly. The great reduction of the number of different pottery shapes that were being produced after the end of the Old Babylonian Period can reasonably be attributed to the presumed hardships of this period.[196]

---

[193] This is because the beginning of Level A XII at Susa is ultimately tied to the chronology of the First Dynasty of Babylon.

[194] GASCHE 1989b, 109-143.

[195] See the comments on the excavation of Babylon in Chapter 2 : Introduction.

[196] On the reduction in the number of pottery shapes, see above p. 26.

As for the goblets, cups, and jars that we have been discussing, several possible scenarios could be proposed for what *might* have happened to them in the period after the fall of Babylon :

1) Potters might have stopped making them, as they did a number of other forms.

2) Potters might have continued producing the vessels ; but the vessels from each part of the country would have begun to acquire local, idiosynchratic characteristics both in their shapes and in their techniques of manufacture. This fragmentation would have been caused by a breakdown in transportion and communication among what was left of the cities. The vessel forms would have continued to evolve, but as the larger unifying tradition came apart, the potters of each area would have gone their own separate ways.

3) Potters might have continued to produce the vessels, and their shapes would have continued to evolve, and that evolution would have taken place within a larger tradition of pottery-making that was still largely coherent. In this situation the changes in vessel shape would have been fairly uniform across a broad region, though such a "region" might have been smaller than it had been in Old Babylonian times.

The first scenario is clearly not true, because the vessels continued to be made. Of the remaining two, Scenario 3 best fits the evidence we have. Changes in shape seem to have been fairly uniform, so that in the latter part of the Early Kassite Period, shapes from ed-Dēr and Nippur look much the same. In spite of the apparent urban retrenchment in early post-Old Babylonian times, the evidence we have been able to assemble indicates that the Babylonian pottery tradition remained coherent. Moreover, in the Early Kassite Period it appears that ceramic manufacturing technology continued to develop with, for example, the increased adoption of the technique to produce filled-in bases for vessels across the whole range of the Kassite ceramic corpus. Unlike the southern Babylonian pottery tradition of the previous century, the northern tradition did not disintegrate, much less disappear. It continued to evolve in a normal way in terms of both the shapes of the vessels that were produced and the ways in which they were manufactured. Moreover, it was during this period of apparent Babylonian weakness that the goblet shape was exported east to Susiana. We therefore infer that the breakdown of the Babylonian state, though significant, was not complete, and further that the period of severest political and social disorder was of relatively short duration. We do not believe that the pottery-making tradition could have survived intact through many decades of instability.

We recognize that trying to understand and explain the historical situation in Babylonia at the beginning of the Early Kassite Period is like trying to construct a picture puzzle with most of the pieces missing. For example, there has not been enough excavation or publication of small and medium-sized Babylonian sites of this period. Since the sites that have been excavated were largely abandoned, we are able to say very little about the social and political life of Babylonia at this time.

We also recognize that in order to find answers to our questions we must look beyond the alluvial plain to the immediately adjacent peripheral regions. Even though conditions were unstable in the core area for some time following the fall of Babylon, urban life apparently continued in outlying areas. In particular, this seems to have been true to the east of the Tigris around

Baghdad.[197] Most significant in this context are the finds from Tell Muḥammad in southeastern Baghdad, where texts and other artifacts from the early post-Old Babylonian era attest to the continuation of settled life and the continuity of the Babylonian ceramic tradition in that region.[198] The archaeological finds from Tell Muḥammad, to be discussed in detail in Chapter 5, reveal that Babylonian or Babylonian-influenced civilization and culture endured on the eastern periphery while in the heartland there was political and social disarray.

The lower Middle Euphrates, too, may have persevered and contributed to the continuity of Babylonian culture. Settlement is known to have continued at least down to the time of Samsuditana,[199] and further exploration of this relatively unknown region may well reveal occupation from the Early Kassite Period. Finally, we must at least mention the Sealand, in southen Babylonia, as a possible contributor to the continuity of Babylonian culture ; however, for the present we can say nothing about this rcgion.

To summarize, our examination of the three most informative pottery forms from the second millennium has shown that there is developmental continuity between their Old Babylonian shapes and their Late Kassite shapes. Moreover, the Late Kassite shapes descend ultimately from the pottery tradition of northern Babylonia as it developed in the Old Babylonian Period. In spite of the deurbanization and unsettled conditions that attended the collapse of the Old Babylonian state in northern Babylonia, the Babylonian pottery-making tradition survived and remained coherent, suggesting that the breakdown of urban-based society in that area was neither total nor of long duration. We hypothesize that the continuance of Babylonian culture depended in part on the continuity of settlement in peripheral areas. At present, the best evidence of such continuity has been disovered east of the Tigris in the region of modern Baghdad.

Most importantly, our examination of Babylonian and peripheral ceramics and archaeological contexts that postdate the collapse of the First Dynasty of Babylon indicates that a chronological scheme much shorter than the Middle Chronology would best fit the available archaeological evidence. Even though the limitations inherent in the available material do not permit a precise date, that material nevertheless suggests that the Middle Chronology is too long by something on the order of 100 years.

---

197 We cannot yet explain the continuity of settlement in the Baghdad region in contrast with northern Babylonia except to offer an environmental explanation. To the extent that northern Babylonia was destabilized in its last decades by floods along the Euphrates (GASCHE 1989b, 140-143), the area east of the Tigris could not have been directly affected.

198 IMAN JAMIL AL-UBAID (1983 [Arabic]).

199 Ahmad Kamel (University of Baghdad) has kindly brought to our attention his MA thesis on Old Babylonian documents found at "Shishun," a site located some 40-50 km south of Ḥīt. Several of these texts are dated to the reign of Samsuditana.

3.

THE TEXTUAL EVIDENCE

Introduction

The reconstruction of Babylonian chronology from textual sources is based upon an amalgamation of information gleaned from kinglists, chronicles, dated administrative documents, and royal inscriptions (particularly those that mention earlier rulers). For the period before the end of the First Dynasty of Babylon, the information about the lengths of kings' reigns that is derived from these sources can be checked against lists of year names.[200] Although year names continued to be used in Babylonia after this time — until at least the reign of Kurigalzu I (c. 1400) and perhaps as late as the reign of Burna-Buriaš II (1359-1333) [201] — there are no lists of year names from the period between the fall of Babylon and the reign of Burna-Buriaš II (by which time scribes had adopted a system of dating years by ordinal numbers within a reign).[202] Moreover, those portions of the native Babylonian chronological sources that pertain to this period are fragmentary. There is also an apparent absence of dated administrative documents against which these sources might be checked. Therefore, Babylonian chronology from the fall of Babylon until the early-to-mid fourteenth century (when significant numbers of dated administrative texts again appear) is enveloped in obscurity. Since Babylonian chronology is ultimately based on synchronisms with Assyrian sources, we will turn to them next.

Before the accession of Sargon II (721-705), Assyrian chronology is based principally upon the Assyrian Kinglist (AKL) tradition.[203] Between 911 and 722 BC, the regnal periods cited in the AKL can be checked against the eponym periods that correspond to them (because we have a continuous sequence of eponyms between 911 and 649).[204] Before 911, however, we have only one fragmentary

---

200 The basic reference remains UNGNAD 1938a ; for subsequent additions and refinements, see especially TAHA BAQIR 1948 and 1949 ; FEIGIN and LANDSBERGER 1955 ; SOLLBERGER 1965, No. 66 ; ARO 1970, No. 8 ; HORSNELL 1974 ; STOL 1976, 2-4 ; DURAND 1977, 17-26 ; SIGRIST 1988 and 1990 ; AR-RAWI 1993. The Sumerian Kinglist, Ur-Isin Kinglist, Larsa Kinglist, and Babylonian Kinglist B record the regnal periods of the kings of the Ur III, Isin I, Larsa, and Babylon I Dynasties, but the figures in these texts are often at variance with the year name data.

201 See BRINKMAN 1976, 402-403. All dates in the introduction to this chapter are cited according to BRINKMAN 1977. The numbers after kings' names, which indicate their positions in dynastic sequences, are also cited according to this source.

202 This system probably began to be used during the reign of Kadašman-Enlil I ([1374]-1360 ; see BRINKMAN 1976, 402-403).

203 Five exemplars of the text are known, only two of which are well preserved (see BRINKMAN 1973, 306, n. 1 ; GRAYSON 1980-83, 101). The latest of the texts ("SDAS" ; see GELB 1954) terminates with the reign of Shalmaneser V (726-722).

204 See MILLARD 1994 ; see also GLASSNER 1993, 161-170, for a translation of the entries corresponding to the period 858-699 BC. The sequence of the eponyms after 649 remains to be established (for a recent survey of the problem and new proposals, see WHITING 1994).

list (*KAV* 21 + 22),[205] which probably commenced with the reign of Tukulti-Ninurta I in the late thirteenth century [206] and supplies also the eponym periods of three kings in the eleventh century (Ashurnasirpal I, Shalmaneser II, and Aššur-nīrārī IV) and one king in the tenth (Tiglath-pileser II).[207] Only one discrepancy between citations of regnal and eponym periods may be significant for the interval between c. 1200 and 912 : Tiglath-pileser II is assigned a 32-year reign in the AKL, while in *KAV* 21 + 22 he is assigned a 33-year reign.[208] Therefore, this portion of the tradition is quite accurate.

The early sections of the AKL, however, have been shown to be less reliable.[209] This is especially true of the portions that list the predecessors of Šamšī-Adad I. For the period after Šamšī-Adad I, there are also discrepancies in citations of genealogies and lengths of reign among the various manuscripts of the AKL ;[210] and none of the regnal lengths cited for the period before the middle of the eleventh century can be verified by other evidence.[211] In addition, there is a virtual absence of documentation in Assyria — apart from approximately two dozen short building inscriptions and labels — between the end of the reign of Šamšī-Adad I and the beginning of the reign of Aššur-nīrārī II (end of the fifteenth century BC).[212]

Nevertheless, there is no body of evidence more important for Mesopotamian chronology between the mid-second millennium and 600 BC than the Assyrian Kinglist tradition. In fact, as J.A. Brinkman has noted, "practically all dates in Mesopotamian history calculated over this time span are based directly or indirectly on the data contained in this tradition."[213] The AKL, therefore — because it provides a continuous sequence of reigns and a nearly continuous sequence of regnal periods over this interval — forms the backbone of Mesopotamian chronology.[214]

---

205 This does not count the fragmentary Mari Eponym Chronicle, which seems to track the career of Šamšī-Adad I (see BIROT 1985, 219-245 ; translated by GLASSNER 1993, 157-160). It has been proposed that the eponym-list fragments published as *KAV* 23 and 24 should be joined with *KAV* 21 + 22 (see MILLARD 1994, 18, A7).

206 POSTGATE 1991, 245.

207 See, respectively, *KAV* 21 iv 4', 17', and 22', and *KAV* 22 v 9''.

208 See, however, BRINKMAN (1973, 310), where it is pointed out that the balance of evidence points in favor of the regnal period attested in the AKL. It should also be noted that the regnal periods of Adad-nīrārī II (911-891) and Tukulti-Ninurta II (890-884) found in the AKL are also at odds with the corresponding eponym periods cited in certain of the eponym lists (BOESE and WILHELM 1979, 19-20 ; for other discrepancies, see POEBEL 1943, 88). These minor discrepancies will be left aside for the present.

209 In a lengthy study published over forty years ago, LANDSBERGER (1954) demonstrated that these portions of the AKL tradition are in conflict with certain royal inscriptions and with the kinglist *KAV* 14, which shows that an alternate line of rulers succeeded Išme-Dagan, son of Šamšī-Adad I. Landsberger also argued that the early sections of the list assign too many generations to a relatively short period of time.

210 See BRINKMAN 1973, 311-314.

211 See, for example, POEBEL 1943, 86-88.

212 GRAYSON 1987, 77-98 ; PEDERSÉN 1985, 29, 89-90 (M9). Significant numbers of texts began to appear only during the reigns of Erība-Adad I and Aššur-uballiṭ I in the fourteenth century (according to SAPORETTI 1979, 29-55).

213 BRINKMAN 1973, 310.

214 The only gap in regnal periods arises from textual damage that has been suffered by all five sources in approximately the same location, which means that the lengths of the reigns of kings 65 and 66 (Aššur-rabi I and Aššur-nādin-aḫḫē I) must be reconstructed. This problem will be addressed below.

Babylonian reigns can be tied to this Assyrian sequence by a network of synchronisms, which are attested in a variety of sources that include (but are not limited to) the synchronistic kinglists, Assyrian royal annals, and the texts known as the Synchronistic History and the Chronicle of Early Kings ; see, in general, BRINKMAN 1976, 28-29 (Kassite Period) ; BRINKMAN 1968, 69-72 (post-Kassite Period) ; BRINKMAN 1972, 272-273 (c. 1500-600).

Hypothesis

We have argued on archaeological grounds that the interval between the fall of Babylon and the beginning of the relatively well-documented phase of the Kassite Dynasty (from c. 1400 BC on) should be reduced. It will now be argued that the chronological sources also allow a reduction. The question is, by how much?

We posit a reduction of some 85-105 years. The most decisive argument in favour of a reduction of this magnitude proceeds from our analysis of the data of the Assyrian Kinglist tradition itself. (The inscriptions of Assyrian kings that contain statements of the time-spans between successive rebuildings of the Aššur and Anu-Adad temples in Assur — *Distanzangaben* — also figure in our analysis but turn out to be much less helpful). Based on premises that will be set forth below, the evidence of the Assyrian Kinglist allows one to calculate approximate dates for the first and last regnal years of Šamšī-Adad I; his reign can then be linked by synchronisms with the reign of Hammurabi and therefore also with the entire ±520-year span from the beginning of Ur III to the fall of Babylon. The methods of reckoning are similar to those employed by previous historians interested in Mesopotamian chronology in the second millennium.[215] However, our approach to the problem differs considerably from those made previously, in that it proceeds from an argument adduced from stratigraphical and ceramic evidence, without the *a priori* assumption that the final result must be made to fit the High-Middle-Low scheme of reckoning. Our goal, it must be stressed, is simply to demonstrate that the textual sources, though often incomplete and difficult to interpret, permit a reduction.

A lower Assyrian chronology of course has implications for Babylonian chronology after 1500 due to the synchronisms that tie the two sequences together.[216] These implications will also be addressed below, after the main argument has been set forth.

3.1. PROCEDURE

3.1.1. *Distanzangaben* and the Date of the Reign of Šamšī-Adad I

Inscriptions of Shalmaneser I, Tiglath-pileser I, and Esarhaddon cite the precise number of years intervening between their respective reconstructions of the main temples in Assur and the work done by previous rulers, going back to the Old Assyrian Period. Unfortunately, these *Distanzangaben* are not renowned for their accuracy because they yield a considerable chronological range within which to place the building activities mentioned in these texts. Nevertheless, because these data have been used repeatedly in the past to reconstruct the chronology of the second millennium, we believe that it is necessary to include them here, even if the results are not entirely conclusive.

In computing these time-spans, the Assyrian scribes will be understood to have started calculating backwards from the actual date at which a temple was rebuilt. The figures given in the inscriptions will be accepted at face value; however, we will also admit the possibility that at least

215 POEBEL 1942a, 289-306, WEIDNER 1945-51, LANDSBERGER 1954, 39-42, and numerous others.

216 Beginning with the link established between Puzur-Aššur III and Burna-Buriaš I in the Assyrian composition known as the Synchronistic History (GRAYSON 1975, 158-159, col. i 5'-7').

one statement telescopes time-spans. These figures will then be employed to establish a range of possible dates for the building activities of Šamšī-Adad I.[217] It must be pointed out in advance that the data in question allow various conclusions, depending on the *a priori* assumptions made. We will make our premises explicit, but a somewhat wider latitude of interpretations is admitted to be possible.

3.1.2. Lunar Calendar vs. Solar Calendar

A recently published analysis of the Middle Assyrian textual sources from Assur and Kār-Tukulti-Ninurta confirms that during the reign of Tiglath-pileser I (No. 87) the lunar calendar, which consisted of 354 days per year, was in use in Assyria.[218] At this time the Babylonian calendar, which contained approximately 365 days, was adopted and an attempt was made to harmonize the two calendars. Both Weidner and Larsen [219] have argued that the lunar calendar was used in Assyria prior to the reign of Tiglath-pileser I. While this has not yet been confirmed by direct evidence, we must point out that before the reign of this king there is no evidence whatsoever of intercalary months in Assyrian texts. This absence of evidence for intercalation does not prove that the Assyrian calendar was based on a lunar cycle before 1114, but we believe — with Weidner and Larsen — that it is likely. This means that we have to subtract one year every 33 years before the reign of Tiglath-pileser I. As an example, we have to deduct 21 years from the time-span between Tiglath-pileser I year 1 (= 1114 BC) and the first year of Šamšī-Adad (= 1813 BC, according to the Middle Chronology).

3.1.3. Assyrian Kinglist Data

Once we have delimited a set of dates for the building activities of Šamšī-Adad I based on the *Distanzangaben* and have translated these into approximate solar dates, the preserved regnal data in the Assyrian Kinglist tradition (presumed to be the most complete and reliable data available) will be used to narrow the range of possibilities. We must first, however, adopt a set of premises to address the issues of variations in regnal periods, the disputed meaning of the term *ṭuppišu* (used to describe several reigns), and the missing regnal periods of Aššur-rabi I (No. 65) and Aššur-nādin-aḫḫē I (No. 66). The task, it must be reiterated, is to narrow the range of possible dates for the reign of Šamšī-Adad I, since the textual data in their present state are insufficient to allow the calculation of absolute dates.

Variants

Because the manuscripts of the AKL [220] exhibit discrepancies in regnal periods, sundry combinations of variants can be employed to calculate the time-range in which Šamšī-Adad's reign should be placed. As a starting point, we will use the higher variants found in BRINKMAN 1977.

---

217 Cf. BOESE and WILHELM 1979, 30 and NA'AMAN 1984, 119.

218 FREYDANK 1991, 81-88. The Assyrian calendar year is thought to have had six months of 30 days plus six months of 29 days (= 354 days).

219 WEIDNER 1935-36, 27-29 ; LARSEN 1976, 193, with n. 5.

220 Three of the five manuscripts are relevant to our discussion (the others exist only in small fragments). We will use the following abbreviations for them, following BRINKMAN (1973, 306, n. 1) : SDAS = Seventh Day Adventist Seminary Kinglist (GELB 1954, 209-230) ; NaKL = Nassouhi Kinglist (NASSOUHI 1927, 1-11) ; and KhKL = Khorsabad Kinglist (GELB 1954, 209-230).

We will then make separate calculations for each list based upon the variants attested in that list alone, using data from the other lists only when a number is broken and must be restored. Thus, the broken number representing the regnal years of Puzur-Aššur III (No. 61) in the Khorsabad list will be restored as either 14 (option 1) or as 24 (option 2).[221] The broken number referring to the regnal period of Aššur-dān I (No. 83) in the Nassouhi list will be restored as 46.[222] The following matrix presents the more significant variants found in the kinglists (to which have been added the numbers favored by BRINKMAN [1977] in his most recent chronological table) :

	KhKL(1)	KhKL(2)	SDAS	NaKL	BRINKMAN (1977)
Aššur-dān I (No. 83) [223]	46	46	46	⌜4⌝6	46
Ninurta-apil-Ekur (No. 82) [224]	3	3	3	13	13
Aššur-nādin-apli (No. 79) [225]	3	3	3	4	4
Puzur-Aššur III (No. 61) [226]	[14]	[24]	24	14	24
total of variants :	66	76	76	77	87

If we accept 46 as the correct number of years for the reign of Aššur-dān I (No. 83) and consider only the variants for the reigns of Puzur-Aššur III (No. 61), Aššur-nādin-apli (No. 79), and Ninurta-apil-Ekur (No. 82), the total of Assyrian regnal years before Aššur-dān I (No. 83), as set forth by BRINKMAN (1977, 343-345), can be reduced by the following intervals :

21 years (if we use a combination of the lowest possible variants from the lists or restore the regnal period of No. 61 in the Khorsabad list as "14") ;

11 years (if we use the variants attested in the SDAS list or restore the regnal period of No. 61 in the Khorsabad list as "24") ;

10 years (if we employ the variants in the Nassouhi list) ; and finally

0 years (if we employ the variants favored by BRINKMAN [1977]).[227]

[221] These are the figures attested, respectively, in the SDAS and Nassouhi lists.

[222] This is the figure attested in both other lists.

[223] The number was read by the original editor as 36 (NASSOUHI 1927, 5, col. "i" 42). However, when BRINKMAN (1973, 309) reexamined the tablet in 1971, he could see only 26([+x]). Nevertheless, BOESE and WILHELM (1979, 23-26) have argued in favor of restoring the number as "36."

[224] KhKL iii 30 ; SDAS iii 17 ; NaKL iii 40. According to BRINKMAN (1973, 313), "[D]espite the current historical fashion which prefers '13' rather than '3' years for the length of the reign of Ninurta-apil-Ekur, it should be pointed out that there is not a single shred of positive evidence in favor of either alternative." Nevertheless, FREYDANK (1991, 29-31, 195) has assigned eleven eponyms to his reign. The evidence that he uses for doing so, however, is circumstantial and seems to be based on the *a priori* assumption of a 13-year reign for this king (see, for example, FREYDANK 1991, 110 [Adad-uballiṭ], 67-69, and n. 190 [Aššur-aḫa-iddina, Bēr-nāṣir, Liptānu, Uzibu], 76-77 [Pišqiya, Ḫabalayu], etc.). Compare SAPORETTI (1979, 133), who assigns no eponyms to this reign.

[225] KhKL iii 22 ; SDAS iii 12 ; NaKL iii 31.

[226] KhKL ii 38 ; SDAS ii 29 ; NaKL ii 35.

[227] Other discrepancies in Assyrian regnal periods, which have been deemed less significant and which will therefore be left out of consideration for the present, include : Aššur-rabi II (No. 95), who is assigned 41 years in KhKL iv 9 and possibly 40 or 41 years (at least 20[+x]) in NaKL iv 23 ; also Tiglath-pileser II (No. 97), who is assigned a 33-year eponym period in the *KAV* 22 v 9'' and a 32-year reign in KhKL iv 13 (with the balance of evidence pointing to the latter). See, in general, BRINKMAN 1973, 310 (collation of NaKL col. iv 23, 28), 311 ; also BOESE and WILHELM 1979, 20.

The apparent discrepancy in the length of reign assigned to Išme-Dagan I (No. 40) in the SDAS list (50 years) and the Khorsabad list (40 years) is based on a misprint in the publication of the former. Both the cast and photo show "40."[228] However, even this lower figure is suspect. The question of how long Išme-Dagan ruled after the death of his father, Šamšī-Adad I, is important to our discussion and will therefore be the topic to which we now turn.

The Duration of the Reign of Išme-Dagan I

The reign of Išme-Dagan I, which according to the AKL began after the death of Šamšī-Adad I and lasted for 40 years, will be reckoned to have lasted only 11 years[229] after the death of the latter.[230] (The demise of Šamšī-Adad can be placed either in Hammurabi year 12, 13, or 17.)[231] New evidence from several Mari letters indicates that Išme-Dagan was forced to vacate the throne of Ekallātum after the invasion of the Elamites (dated Zimri-Līm year 9' = Hammurabi 28)[232] and to seek exile at Hammurabi's court in Babylon.[233] Thereupon, Atamrum, an Elamite proxy, is said to have instigated a conspiracy in Ekallātum to place Išme-Dagan's son, Mut-Aškur, on the throne in his stead.[234] Išme-Dagan, who is said to have been gravely ill and uncertain to recover (*murṣam rabêm maruṣ balāssu ul kīn*), is not attested again after Zimri-Līm year 11' (= Hammurabi 30).[235] According to the kinglist *KAV* 14, Mut-Aškur in fact did succeed Išme-Dagan as king, initiating a second line of rulers in Assyria (Nos. 40a-c) that ran contemporaneously with part or all of the line represented by Aššur-dugul and his successors (Nos. 41-53).[236] The former line may have reigned in Ekallātum and the latter in Assur.[237]

---

228 J.A. Brinkman, pers. comm.

229 This figure of 11 years is based on the supposition that Šamšī-Adad died in Hammurabi year 17 and that the reign of Išme-Dagan I ended in Hammurabi year 28. For the argument, see below.

230 This is similar to the position taken by LANDSBERGER (1954, 36-37), who suggested that Išme-Dagan's 40-year reign included a period of approximately 20 years during which he acted as viceroy in Ekallātum (before his father's death) and approximately 20 years during which he acted as king of Assyria (after his father's death). VEENHOF (1985, 212) also noted that 40 is a "suspiciously long and round figure" and suggested that it probably includes the years when Išme-Dagan ruled as viceroy.

231 CHARPIN and DURAND (1985, 306-308 ; see also VEENHOF 1985, 217-218) have argued that the death of Šamšī-Adad occurred in Hammurabi year 17 = Ibâl-pī-El 4 (= 1776 BC, Middle Chronology). However, WHITING (1990, 310, n. 205) has objected to the conclusions of Charpin and Durand on several grounds, and prefers the traditional date of Hammurabi 12 ([or 13] = 1781 [or 1780] BC, Middle Chronology) for the death of Šamšī-Adad. For the sake of argument, we opt to accept the date proposed by Charpin and Durand.

232 For the dating of the Elamite invasion to ZL 9', see CHARPIN 1987 and 1986 ; DURAND 1986, 122, 128 ; and CHARPIN and DURAND 1991. According to Charpin, the Elamites, allied with Zimri-Līm and Hammurabi, took Ešnunna at the beginning of the year ZL 9', and shortly thereafter captured the banks of the Tigris and made Išme-Dagan I a vassal. DURAND (1986, 118 ; and 1995, 18) argues that the attack on Ešnunna took place at end of ZL 8' (= "Year when Zimri-Līm sent auxiliary forces to Elam" [an event that actually took place in the preceding year]).

233 CHARPIN *et al.* 1988, 154-156.

234 CHARPIN *et al.* 1988, 155.

235 CHARPIN *et al.* 1988, 155-156 (the reference to Išme-Dagan's illness and its prognosis is found in CHARPIN *et al.* 1988, No. 371 : 40-42) ; cf. BIROT 1978, 186. VEENHOF (1985, 213) has proposed that Išme-Dagan's final year was Hammurabi 31.

236 GRAYSON 1980-83, 115 ; BRINKMAN 1977, 344 ; LANDSBERGER 1954, 31. According to VEENHOF (1985, 213), Mut-Aškur would have ascended the throne sometime in the period between Hammurabi years 31 and 33. It is unclear where Puzur-Sîn (No. 40d according to Landsberger) should be placed in this scheme. According to his own inscription, he followed Asīnum (No. 40c), but whether he followed directly afterwards or not cannot be determined at present (GRAYSON 1985, 9-14 ; 1987, 77-78).

237 Asīnum (No. 40c) also seems to have exercised authority in Assur, inasmuch as Puzur-Sîn credited him with doing work on the palace of his (Asīnum's) grandfather, Šamšī-Adad (GRAYSON 1985, 12 ; 1989, 77-78). The monarchy in Assyria appears to have become united again only under Šū-Ninūa (No. 54).

If we accept that Išme-Dagan I ruled for only 11 years after the death of Šamšī-Adad I, and not 40 years, a reduction is required in our calculation of the time-range in which the reign of the latter should be placed. The magnitude of reduction would be

29 years.

The Meaning of ṭuppišu

The term *ṭuppišu*, which in the AKL is used to describe the reigns of kings 42-47 (Aššur-apla-idi through Adasi) and 84-85 (Ninurta-tukulti-Aššur and Mutakkil-Nusku), will be understood to refer, respectively, to the last regnal years of kings 41 (Aššur-dugul) and 83 (Aššur-dān I). This is the most plausible interpretation of *ṭuppu*, especially in the context of the AKL's description of the reigns of kings 42-46, of whom it is said : *ina tarṣi Aššur-dugul mar la mammana* ... 6 *šarrani mar lā mammana bāb ṭuppišu šarrūta īpuš*, "In the time of Aššur-dugul, son of a nobody ... 6 kings, sons of nobodies, exercised kingship (at the) beginning of his *ṭuppu*."[238] (In chronological reckoning, *ṭuppišu* has been understood by most modern interpreters to equal either 0 years,[239] 0-1 year,[240] or 1 year.)[241]

W. von Soden (*AHw*, 1379-80) has connected this term with the verb *ṭapāpu*, which, on the basis of the contexts in which it is used and especially the synonyms with which it is associated, means "to be very full." The principal synonyms in question are *malû* and *šebû*, which are used to describe the process of reaching the end of a time-span. Therefore, the term *ṭuppišu*, as employed in the AKL, can be understood to mean "(at) the end of his (the previous king's) reign."

We believe that recently published evidence supports the interpretation of *ṭuppu* as the portion of a deceased ruler's final regnal year that was completed by his successor (thus, in chronological reckoning = 0 years). In an eighth-century inscription, Ninurta-kudurrī-uṣur, governor of Sūḫu and Mari, after introducing his genealogy and call to high office by the gods, states that :

> 3 ITI.MEŠ *ina muḫḫi ṭuppišu*[242] *ina rēš šakin-mātūtiya ša ina kussi ša abiya ūšibu 2 līm* LÚ *Ḫatallu ultu* LÚ *Sarūgu adi* LÚ *Luḫuāyu itti ṣābī qašti u šūt rēš karašišunu ipḫurūma ṭēmī ana aḫāmeš iškunūma,*
>
> Three months into his (i.e., my father's) *ṭuppu*, at the beginning of my governorship, when I occupied the throne of my father, 2000 Ḫatallu tribesmen — from the Sarūgu clan

---

238 GRAYSON 1980-83, 106 § 15. The term *bābu*,"opening," is used in Old Assyrian documents to mean "beginning" (see *AHw* 95 sub *bābu(m)* I 9). The word may also mean "before." Regardless of whether *bāb ṭuppišu* should be interpreted as "(at the) beginning of his *ṭuppu*" or "before his *ṭuppu*," kings 42-46 claimed kingship during the reign of Aššur-dugul, and therefore their combined reigns have to be reckoned as 0 years.

239 POEBEL 1942a, 296, n. 130 ; 1943, 61, 65 ; ROWTON 1946, 100-101 ; 1951, 197-201 ; 1959a, 9, n. 40 ; 1959b, 213-222 ; 1970, 203 ; HORNUNG 1964, 44, and n. 17 ; and VAN DER MEER 1963, 10-11.

240 CAVAIGNAC 1955, 206 and BOESE and WILHELM 1979, 35, 38.

241 WEIDNER 1945-51, 86. It should be noted, however, that SMITH (1945, 19-20), LANDSBERGER (1949, 268-272, 1954, 38, n. 38), CORNELIUS (1954-56, 296), and TADMOR (1958, 135-136) understood *ṭuppišu* to designate a reign of unknown duration (cf. also BRINKMAN 1973, 313).

242 The suffix *-šu*, "his," which has no apparent antecedent in the text, can only be understood in the context to refer to the term *abiya*, "my father," which is introduced shortly afterwards. There is a close parallel in usage in *ABL* 447 rev. 18-20 : *annûte* 3 *ša adi ṭuppišu iškaru ugammarūni*, "These are the three who are completing the series to its fullest extent."

to the Luḫuāyu clan, with archers and their camp commanders — gathered and came to an agreement about a joint course of action.[243]

From this passage it is evident that the beginning of the governorship of Ninurta-kudurrī-uṣur (*rēš šakin-mātūti*) [244] overlapped and may have been coterminous with the interval described as the *ṭuppu* of his predecessor, which had begun three months earlier. Therefore, we will calculate *ṭuppišu* as :

0 years.[245]

Regnal Years of Aššur-rabi I (No. 65) and Aššur-nādin-aḫḫē I (No. 66)

The combined reigns of kings 65 and 66 (missing in AKL) will be calculated to have been 29 years (i.e., 14 + 15).[246] This figure is an approximation, derived from calculations of the average throne tenure of kings 55-64 and 67-76 (= 14.4 years when the lower variant for the reign of Puzur-Aššur III [No. 61] is used [i.e., 14 years], and = 14.9 years when the higher variant for the reign of Puzur-Aššur III is used [i.e., 24 years]).[247]

Their reigns are unlikely to have lasted longer. The period during which they ruled was marked by instability in the monarchy. According to the extant sources, Aššur-rabi I (No. 65) deposed Aššur-šadûni (No. 64), his nephew, after the latter had reigned for only one month, and Enlil-nāṣir II (No. 67) deposed Aššur-nādin-aḫḫē I (No. 66), his brother, after [x] year(s).[248] Also, the reigns of kings 67-70 were all of short duration — respectively 6 years, 7 years, 9 years, and 8 years — indicating continuing volatility. This question is addressed in a different context below.

3.2. The Middle Chronology in Light of the Assyrian Kinglist Tradition

Before we proceed further, it is important to examine the evidence of the AKL, which underpins the entire second-millennium chronological sequence, to determine how well it fits the Middle Chronology scheme. It is our contention that it can be made to fit only if unusually long reigns are assigned to kings 65 and 66 (whose regnal periods, it will be recalled, are missing in the AKL), and that therefore a shorter chronology is indicated.

For the sake of argument, let us assume that Išme-Dagan I reigned for 40 years following the death of Šamšī-Adad I (which in light of the foregoing evidence seems improbable). Let us also assume that the broken figure in the Khorsabad Kinglist referring to the reign of Puzur-Aššur III

243 CAVIGNEAUX and ISMAIL 1990, 343, col. i 7-11 ; FRAME 1995, 295, col. i 7-11.

244 The phrase *rēš šakin-mātūti* is otherwise unattested, but it clearly parallels *rēš šarrūti*, which refers to the beginning of a king's reign.

245 It should be noted that in the case of the reigns of Ninurta-tukulti-Aššur (No. 84) and Mutakkil-Nusku (No. 85), BRINKMAN (1977, 345) has apparently also interpreted *ṭuppišu* as 0 years.

246 POEBEL (1942a, 289-296 ; 1943, 86) calculated their combined regnal years as 0.

247 NA'AMAN (1984, 118) computed their combined reigns as either 31 and 32 years.

248 GRAYSON 1980-83, 108 §§ 32-35. It may have been during this era or slightly before that Sauštatar, ruler of Mitanni, raided Assur and carried away to Wašukanni a silver and gold door, as reported in the text of a treaty concluded in the following century between Šattiwaza and the Hittite king Šuppiluliuma (WEIDNER 1923, 38, No. 2 : 8-9).

(No. 61) should be restored as [24] (the higher variant attested in the SDAS list). And finally, let us assume that the broken number in the Nassouhi Kinglist referring to the reign of Aššur-dān I (No. 83) should be restored as 46 (the variant attested in both KhKL and SDAS). These variants are reproduced below for ease of reference :

	KhKL(1)	KhKL(2)	SDAS	NaKL	BRINKMAN (1977)
Aššur-dān I (No. 83)	46	46	46	⸢4⸣6	46
Ninurta-apil-Ekur (No. 82)	3	3	3	13	13
Aššur-nādin-apli (No. 79)	3	3	3	4	4
Puzur-Aššur III (No. 61)	[14]	[24]	24	14	24
total of variants :	66	76	76	77	87

If we use the figures representing the total of variants and combine them with the known lengths of reign between the first year of Tiglath-pileser I (1114-1076) and the first year of Šamšī-Adad I (traditionally set at 1813-1781), we arrive at dates of 1716 + x, 1726 + x, 1727 + x, and 1737 + x (where x = the combined years of kings 65 + 66) as possibilities for the first regnal year of Šamšī-Adad, depending on which set of variants we employ.[249] In order to harmonize these dates with the traditional Middle Chronology date for Šamšī-Adad's first year (1813), we must conclude that kings 65 and 66 (whose regnal periods are missing in the AKL) reigned for a combination of, respectively, 97 years (i.e., 1813 minus 1716 years [KhKL(1)]), 87 years (i.e., 1813 minus 1726 years [KhKL(2), SDAS]), 86 years (1813 minus 1727 [NaKL]), or 76 years (1813 minus 1737 [Brinkman]). These figures are probably too high.

The problem can be illuminated another way.

Kings 63-68, who were all sons or grandsons of Enlil-nāṣir I (No. 62), reigned a total of 25 (= 7 + 6 + 12) + x years.[250] The following schema represents their genealogical affiliation :

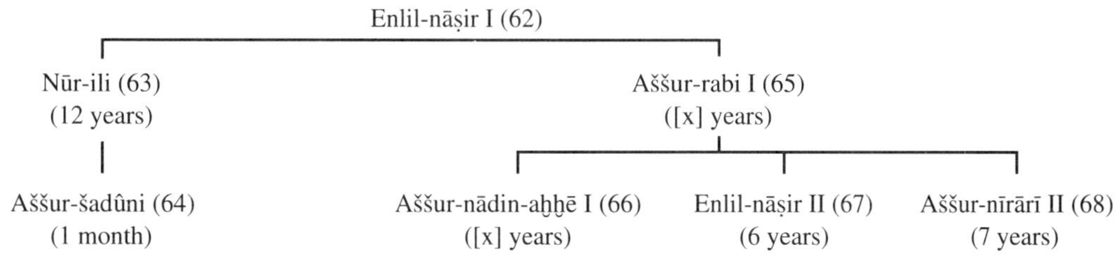

249 It should be noted that the Nassouhi List is fragmentary ; therefore we do not know whether or not it originally exhibited other variants. The calculations above are based upon the assumption that the Nassouhi List agreed with KhKL and SDAS with regard to the other regnal periods between Šamšī-Adad I and Tiglath-pileser I.

250 See, in general, GRAYSON 1980-83, 108-109 §§ 32-36. According to the AKL, Nūr-ili (No. 63) and Aššur-rabi I (No. 65) were sons of Enlil-nāṣir I (No. 62) and reigned, respectively, *12 years* and [*x*] *years*. Aššur-šadûni (No. 64), Aššur-nādin-aḫḫē I (No. 66), and Enlil-nāṣir II (No. 67) were grandsons of Enlil-nāṣir I (No. 62) and reigned, respectively, *1 month*, [*x*] *years*, and *6 years*. Aššur-nīrārī II (No. 68) was also a grandson of Enlil-nāṣir I (No. 62). This is according to the evidence of the inscriptions of the kings Aššur-rēʾim-nišēšu (No. 70 [GRAYSON 1987, 101 : 3-4]), Erība-Adad I (No. 72 [GRAYSON 1987, 107 : 8-9]), and Aššur-uballiṭ I (No. 73 [GRAYSON 1987, 110 : 7-8]). In these inscriptions, Aššur-nīrārī II (No. 68) is stated to have been the son of Aššur-rabi I (No. 65), and not, as the AKL indicates, the son of Enlil-nāṣir II (No. 67 [the latter was in fact his brother]). Aššur-nīrārī II (No. 68) reigned *7 years*, if we accept the evidence of the Assyrian Kinglist tradition.

If we accept that the Middle Chronology is correct, and that therefore the unknown duration of rule of kings 65 and 66 (= x) must amount to 97, 87, 86, or 76 years, as demonstrated, then the royal careers of the sons and grandsons of Enlil-nāṣir I must have spanned, respectively, a total of 122 years (= 25 + 97), 112 years (= 25 + 87), 111 years (= 25 + 86), or 101 years (= 25 + 76). That two generations of kings could have occupied the throne for so long is possible but unlikely, especially in light of the instability in throne tenure that is evident during this era. As we have already emphasized, the extant sources state that Aššur-rabi I (No. 65) deposed Aššur-šadûni (No. 64), his nephew, after the latter had reigned for only one month, and Enlil-nāṣir II (No. 67) deposed Aššur-nādin-aḫḫē I (No. 66), his brother, after [x] year(s).[251]

Finally, if the combined period of rule of kings 63-68 spanned more than a century, one wonders why only three texts can be reliably dated to the era.[252] In sharp contrast, there are scores of texts that can be assigned to the periods immediately before and after.[253] The paucity of epigraphic finds attributable to kings 63-68 may be due to the vagaries of archaeological discovery or to the interference of Mitanni,[254] but we would argue that it results more from the artificial length of the Middle Chronology. A lower chronology would better fit the evidence.

3.3. A Plausible Lower Chronology

The stratigraphic and ceramic evidence presented above in Chapter 2 argues strongly for a reduction of "something on the order of 100 years" in the chronology of Mesopotamia before c. 1400. The task before us now is to find a set of credible alternatives to the Middle Chronology that both congrue with the archaeological evidence and can be harmonized with the chronological data found in the texts. (This field of candidates can be narrowed by astronomical dating ; see Chapter 4.) As already stated, our approach differs significantly from all previous approaches to the problem, in that it proceeds from an argument that a lower chronology would much better fit the archaeological evidence now available.

---

251 GRAYSON 1980-83, 108 §§ 32-35.

252 The texts in question are a fragmentary clay cone of Aššur-rabi I (GRAYSON 1987, 98), a document recording a royal donation made by Aššur-nīrārī II (PEDERSÉN 1985, 94-95 [No. 16 = *KAJ* 177] ; SAPORETTI 1979, 29), and a loan document that can also be dated to the latter's reign (PEDERSÉN 1985, 90 [No. 75 = *KAJ* 28]). However, it should be noted that some of the inscriptions that Grayson (1987, 83-117) has assigned to the span between Šamšī-Adad III (No. 59) and Enlil-nāṣir I (No. 62), as well as to the span between Aššur-bēl-nišēšu (No. 69) and Erība-Adad I (No. 72), are too fragmentary to attribute to specific rulers and may therefore belong to the period in question. It is also possible that the brick inscriptions that he has assigned to Aššur-nādin-aḫḫē II (No. 71) should be attributed rather to Aššur-nādin-aḫḫē I (No. 66).

253 From the period before, over 40 individual inscriptions can be securely assigned to the five or six decades extending from the beginning of the reign of Aššur-nīrārī I (No. 60) to the reign of Enlil-nāṣir I (No. 62). From the period after, more than 20 individual inscriptions (and at least two dozen other documents) can be dated to the 90-year span from the beginning of the reign of Aššur-bēl-nišēšu (No. 69) through the reign of Aššur-uballiṭ I (No. 73 ; see GRAYSON 1987, 83-117 ; SAPORETTI 1979, 29-35).

254 Sauštatar's raid on Assur (see n. 248 above) has been taken as evidence that the kingdom of Mitanni took control of the city at this time. We should not be surpised if Mitanni thereafter meddled in Assyrian affairs, especially in its monarchical succession.

3.3.1. The Assyrian *Distanzangaben*

Our analysis of the *Distanzangaben* makes it apparent that no firm chronological conclusions can be drawn from them. The statements of Shalmaneser I can be interpreted to support either the High Chronology or a chronology that is even lower than the one that we would suggest; Tiglath-pileser I's statements yield dates that are in the range of the Middle Chronology; while those of Esarhaddon yield dates that support our contention that the Middle Chronology is too high. In view of the discrepancies resulting from these data, we feel it is necessary to probe this information.

Shalmaneser I

Shalmaneser (No. 77) claims in various inscriptions that he rebuilt Eḫursagkurkurra, the temple of Aššur, after a fire had destroyed it. In two texts, he specifies the number of years before his own rebuilding that other construction projects had been undertaken in the complex.[255] It may be helpful to quote the principal text:[256]

> When Eḫursagkurkurra — the temple of Aššur my lord, which Ušpiya, vice-regent of Aššur, my forefather, had previously built — became dilapidated, Ērišu, my forefather, vice-regent of Aššur rebuilt (it). From the reign of Ērišu 159 years passed and the temple (again) became dilapidated and Šamšī-Adad, vice-regent of Aššur rebuilt (it). 580 years passed and that temple which Šamšī-Adad, vice-regent of Aššur, had rebuilt became extremely old. Fire broke out in it. The temple ... (and) all the property of the temple of Aššur, my lord, was consumed in the fire [Shalmaneser then describes how he rebuilt the temple].

Shalmaneser states first that 159 years had elapsed between Ērišu I's rebuilding and the rebuilding undertaken by Šamšī-Adad I (the terminus of the interval being Šamšī-Adad's final year).[257] He then states that "580 years passed and that temple which Šamšī-Adad, vice-regent of Aššur, had rebuilt became extremely old," fire destroyed it, and he rebuilt it.

The above-quoted text allows another interpretation. The 580-year period may also be understood to refer to the number of years that passed between Ērišu's rebuilding and that done by Shalmaneser. In this case the 159-year period between Ērišu and Šamšī-Adad was included in the 580-year span. If so, 421 years had elapsed between the final year of Šamšī-Adad and Shalmaneser's reconstruction.

255 GRAYSON 1987, 185, lines 112-148; 189, lines 5-21. The two texts in question are inscribed, respectively, on nearly two dozen stone tablets and five dozen clay cones uncovered from the temple and its surrounding area.

256 GRAYSON 1987, 185, lines 112-128.

257 The assertion is based on comparison with the statement of Esarhaddon in his Assur A inscription, wherein he records that 126 years had elapsed between these rebuildings (see below). The difference between the figure given by Shalmaneser I (159) and the figure given by Esarhaddon (126) is 33 years — i.e., exactly the number of years attributed to the reign of Šamšī-Adad in the AKL. Therefore, the scribes of Shalmaneser I computed their figure based on the end of Šamšī-Adad's reign; the scribes of Esarhaddon computed their figure based on its beginning.

Unfortunately, the date that Shalmaneser used as a base of reckoning is unknown, otherwise we could simply add 580 or 421 years to it and compute possible dates for Šamšī-Adad's final year. These dates, however, can be approximately determined on the basis of Esarhaddon's statement that Shalmaneser's reconstruction work was accomplished 586 or 580 years before his own rebuilding in 679 BC (see below). When we add these figures (i.e., 586/580 + 679), we arrive at 1265 or 1259 BC for Shalmaneser's rebuilding. Adding first 580 years, then 421 years, the final year of Šamšī-Adad is calculated to have been

1845 BC (= 679 + 586 + 580)
or
1839 BC (= 679 + 580 + 580)
or
1686 BC (= 679 + 586 + 421)
or
1680 BC (= 679 + 580 + 421).

Finally, when we correct these dates against the solar calendar, we arrive at the following possible dates for Šamšī-Adad's last regnal year :

1823 BC (= 1845 minus the 22 years [solar correction] that are assumed to have accrued over the period between 1845 and the reign of Tiglath-pileser I),
or
1817 BC (= 1839 minus 22 years [solar correction]),
or
1669 BC (= 1686 minus 17 years [solar correction]),
or
1663 BC (= 1680 minus 17 years [solar correction]).

Because the last two dates calculated on the basis of Shalmaneser's *Distanzangaben* are so low, we posit that the scribes responsible for his inscriptions assigned an 11-year reign to Išme-Dagan I. We will also assume, for the sake of argument, that both Shalmaneser's and Esarhaddon's scribes may have consulted versions of the kinglist (or eponym lists) in which were entered only the low variants for the reigns of Puzur-Aššur III (No. 61), Aššur-nādin-apli (No. 79), and Ninurta-apil-Ekur (No. 82). On this assumption, the above dates for the final year of Šamšī-Adad I could have been as much as 21 years higher. Therefore, the following are also proposed as possibilities :

1690 BC
or
1684 BC.

Tiglath-pileser I

Tiglath-pileser (No. 87) claimed to have initiated reconstruction of the Anu-Adad temple in Assur in his accession year (1115 BC). The account of his rebuilding, which is found in the first edition of his annals (dated perhaps to 1109 BC),[258] also contains statements of the time-spans that had elapsed between previous construction activities and his own.

Tiglath-pileser first states that 641 years had passed from the time that Šamšī-Adad built the temple of Anu and Adad to the time that it became dilapidated.[259] He then states that Aššur-dān (No. 83) tore it down, and that for 60 years its foundations remained unlaid. Finally, as mentioned already, Tiglath-pileser claims to have started rebuilding the temple upon his accession to the throne in 1115.

These statements yield only one date upon which we can base calculations of the date of Šamšī-Adad's original construction of the Anu-Adad temple : 1175 BC (= 1115 + 60). When we add 641 years to 1175, we arrive at the following possible date for his work :

1816 BC.

Correcting this date against the solar calendar (remembering that the lunar calendar is posited to have been in use in Assyria before the reign of Tiglath-pileser I), we arrive at the following figure :

1795 BC (= 1816 –21 years [solar correction]).

Finally, for the sake of argument, we will assume that the versions of the AKL that assign 40 years to the reign of Išme-Dagan I (No. 40) had come into being by then.[260] If the scribes of Tiglath-pileser had consulted such a source (or sources), they would have assigned 29 more years to his reign than is probably justified (since Išme-Dagan I is understood to have reigned for only 11 years after the death of Šamšī-Adad I, not 40). Therefore, the following is also a possible date for Šamšī-Adad's reconstruction of the Anu-Adad temple :

1767 BC (= 1816 minus 29 minus 20 [solar correction]).

Depending on which variants were used, these dates may also be as much as 21 years higher or lower.

Esarhaddon

Esarhaddon also claims to have rebuilt the temple of Aššur.[261] In an inscription labeled by the modern editor as Assur A, Esarhaddon states that 129 years had elapsed between Ērišu's rebuilding and that accomplished by Šamšī-Adad I. (Šamšī-Adad's reconstruction is seemingly reckoned as having been completed in his first regnal year.) [262] Another 434 years are then said to have passed, at

---

258 GRAYSON 1991, 28, col. vii 60-114.

259 The text errs in calling Šamšī-Adad the son of Išme-Dagan. Šamšī-Adad I (No. 39) is obviously meant here, not Šamšī-Adad III (No. 59) — this is not only because Šamšī-Adad I is the only earlier king to whom we may confidently attribute work on this complex (cf. GRAYSON 1987, 80-81, A.0.59.1001), but also because Šamšī-Adad III cannot possibly have ruled 641 years before Tiglath-pileser I.

260 The latest significant redaction of the kinglist probably took place in Middle Assyrian times (or very early in the Neo-Assyrian Period ; see BRINKMAN 1973, 315).

261 BORGER 1956, 3-5, col. iii 16-vi 27 (Ass. A) ; 6-7, lines 19-47 (Ass. B).

262 See n. 257 above.

which time the temple burned down and Shalmaneser I rebuilt it. Finally, another interval of 580 years passed (586 years according to Assur B), and Esarhaddon undertook the temple's rennovation.

Since the Assur A inscription is dated to 679 BC (i.e., in the eponymy of Issi-Adad-anīnu), we take this year as our base of reckoning (and Esarhaddon's). Totaling the intervals in question (679 + 586/580 + 434), we arrive at the following possible dates for Šamšī-Adad's rebuilding of the Aššur temple :

1699 BC,
or
1693 BC.

Corrected against solar dates, these translate into :

1682 BC (= 1699 minus 17 years [solar correction for the period 1699-1115]),
or
1676 BC (= 1693 minus 17 years [solar correction]).

Since the scribes of Esarhaddon would have had at their disposal a regnal list assigning a 40-year reign to Išme-Dagan I (e.g., the Khorsabad list, copied from an Assur original and dated to 738 BC), the above dates are perhaps 29 years too high (based on our premise that Išme-Dagan's reign lasted only 11 years after the death of his father).

A 29-year reduction, however, would result in a chronology too low to be harmonized with the post-1500 dates established on the basis of Assyrian-Babylonian(-Egyptian) synchronisms (and ultimately anchored by the solar eclipse of 763). Therefore, we will also consider Landsberger's suggestion that the interval of 434 years (7 *šūši* + 14), cited in Assur A as the period between Šamšī-Adad's and Shalmaneser's rebuildings, is a scribal error and should be corrected to 494 years (8 *šūši* + 14).[263] Admitting this as a possibility, when we total the intervals again, then subtract 29 years (on the premise that Esarhaddon's scribes assigned 40 years to Išme-Dagan I instead of 11 years), and finally correct the achieved results against the solar calendar (subtracting 18 years this time instead of 17), we arrive at the following dates for Šamšī-Adad's rebuilding :

1712 BC (679 + 586 + 494 minus 29 minus 18),
or
1706 BC (679 + 580 + 494 minus 29 minus 18).

Summary of the Distanzangaben *Analysis*

Based on the *Distanzangaben* data found in the inscriptions of Shalmaneser I, Tiglath-pileser I, and Esarhaddon, we have calculated a range of dates in which the temple-building activities of Šamšī-Adad I can possibly be placed. This range extends from 1845 to 1663 BC. The following

[263] LANDSBERGER 1954, 40.

is a summary of the dates calculated on this basis (* = possible first year of Šamšī-Adad ; and ** = possible final year) :

Year	*King*	*Base of reckoning*	*Factors in calculation*		*Solar correction*
1663**	Shalm. I	679 +	580 (Esarh—Shalm) + 421 (Shalm—Š-A)		–17
1669**	Shalm. I	679 +	586 (Esarh—Shalm) + 421 (Shalm—Š-A)		–17
1676*	Esarh.	679 +	580 (Esarh—Shalm) + 434 (Shalm—Š-A)		–17
1680**	Shalm. I	679 +	580 (Esarh—Shalm) + 421 (Shalm—Š-A)		lunar date
1682*	Esarh.	679 +	586 (Esarh—Shalm) + 434 (Shalm—Š-A)		–17
1684**	Shalm. I	679 +	580 (Esarh—Shalm) + 421 (Shalm—Š-A)	+ 21 (high variants)	–17
1686**	Shalm. I	679 +	586 (Esarh—Shalm) + 421 (Shalm—Š-A)		lunar date
1690**	Shalm. I	679 +	586 (Esarh—Shalm) + 421 (Shalm—Š-A)	+ 21 (high variants)	–17
1693*	Esarh.	679 +	580 (Esarh—Shalm) + 434 (Shalm—Š-A)		lunar date
1699*	Esarh.	679 +	586 (Esarh—Shalm) + 434 (Shalm—Š-A)		lunar date
1706*	Esarh.	679 +	580 (Esarh—Shalm) + 494 (Shalm—Š-A)	– 29 (Iš-D)	–18
1712*	Esarh.	679 +	586 (Esarh—Shalm) + 494 (Shalm—Š-A)	– 29 (Iš-D)	–18
1767	T-p I	1115 +	60 (T-p—Aš-d) + 641 (Aš-d—Š-A)	– 29 (Iš-D)	–20
1795	T-p I	1115 +	60 (T-p—Aš-d) + 641 (Aš-d—Š-A)		–21
1816	T-p I	1115 +	60 (T-p—Aš-d) + 641 (Aš-d—Š-A)		lunar date
1817**	Shalm. I	679 +	580 (Esarh—Shalm) + 580 (Shalm—Š-A)		–22
1823**	Shalm. I	679 +	586 (Esarh—Shalm) + 580 (Shalm—Š-A)		–22
1839**	Shalm. I	679 +	580 (Esarh—Shalm) + 580 (Shalm—Š-A)		lunar date
1845**	Shalm. I	679 +	586 (Esarh—Shalm) + 580 (Shalm—Š-A)		lunar date

As stated at the beginning of this section, the *Distanzangaben* cannot be used with any degree of confidence in establishing accurate dates for the reign of Šamšī-Adad. We therefore turn to the Assyrian Kinglist data to see how much help they provide in reconstructing the chronology of the period with which we are concerned.

3.3.2. The Assyrian Kinglist Data

All calculations based on these data will be guided by the premises set forth in Sections 3.1.2 and 3.1.3. We will first establish a base chronology, using the higher variants for the reigns of Puzur-Aššur III (No. 61), Aššur-nādin-apli (No. 79), Ninurta-apil-Ekur (No. 82), and Aššur-dān I (No. 83), following BRINKMAN (1977, 345). The reign of Išme-Dagan I will be reckoned as 11 years ; *ṭuppišu* will be reckoned as 0 years ; and the combined reigns of Aššur-rabi I (No. 65) and Aššur-nādin-aḫḫē I (No. 66) will be set at 29 years. This base chronology will then be corrected against solar dates. By our reckoning, it is possible to place the reign of Šamšī-Adad almost one century later than it is presently located within the framework of the Middle Chronology.

Base Chronology

87.	Tiglath-pileser I	1114-1076	(39)
86.	Aššur-rēša-iši I	1132-1115	(18)
85.	Mutakkil-Nusku	1133	*ṭuppišu*
84.	Ninurta-tukulti-Aššur	1133	*ṭuppišu*
83.	Aššur-dān I	1178-1133	(46)
82.	Ninurta-apil-Ekur	1191-1179	(13) var. 3
81.	Enlil-kudurrī-uṣur	1196-1192	(5)
80.	Aššur-nīrārī III	1202-1197	(6)
79.	Aššur-nādin-apli	1206-1203	(4) var. 3
78.	Tukulti-Ninurta I	1243-1207	(37)
77.	Shalmaneser I	1273-1244	(30)
76.	Adad-nīrārī I	1305-1274	(32)
75.	Arik-dēn-ili	1317-1306	(12)
74.	Enlil-nīrārī	1327-1318	(10)
73.	Aššur-uballiṭ I	1363-1328	(36)
72.	Erība-Adad I	1390-1364	(27)
71.	Aššur-nādin-aḫḫē II	1400-1391	(10)
70.	Aššur-rē'im-nišēšu	1408-1401	(8)
69.	Aššur-bēl-nišēšu	1417-1409	(9)
68.	Aššur-nīrārī II	1424-1418	(7)
67.	Enlil-nāṣir II	1430-1425	(6)
66.	Aššur-nādin-aḫḫē I	*1445-1431*	[*15**]
65.	Aššur-rabi I	*1459-1446*	[*14**]
64.	Aššur-šadûni	1459	(1 mo.)
63.	Nūr-ili	1471-1460	(12)
62.	Enlil-nāṣir I	1484-1472	(13)
61.	Puzur-Aššur III	1508-1485	(24) var. 14
60.	Aššur-nīrārī I	1534-1509	(26)
59.	Šamšī-Adad III	1550-1535	(16)
58.	Išme-Dagan II	1566-1551	(16)
57.	Šamšī-Adad II	1572-1567	(6)
56.	Ērišu III	1585-1573	(13)
55.	Šarma-Adad II	1588-1586	(3)
54.	Šū-Ninūa	1602-1589	(14)

53.	Lullaya	1608-1603	(6)		
52.	Bazaya	1636-1609	(28)		
51.	IB.TAR-Sîn	1648-1637	(12)		
50.	Šarma-Adad I	1660-1649	(12)		
49.	Libbaya	1677-1661	(17)		
48.	Bēlu-bāni	1687-1678	(10)		
47.	Adasi	1688	*ina tarṣi Aššur-dugul . . . bāb ṭuppišu*		
46.	Adad-ṣalūlu	1688	*ina tarṣi Aššur-dugul . . . bāb ṭuppišu*		
45.	Ipqi-Ištar	1688	*ina tarṣi Aššur-dugul . . . bāb ṭuppišu*		
44.	Sîn-namir	1688	*ina tarṣi Aššur-dugul . . . bāb ṭuppišu*		
43.	Nāṣir-Sîn	1688	*ina tarṣi Aššur-dugul . . . bāb ṭuppišu*	41c.	Asīnum
42.	Aššur-apla-idi	1688	*ina tarṣi Aššur-dugul . . . bāb ṭuppišu*	41b.	Rimu-x
41.	Aššur-dugul	1693-1688	(6)	41a.	Mut-Aškur

40.	Išme-Dagan I	1704-1694	(11)
39.	Šamšī-Adad I	**1737-1705**	(33)

Išme-Dagan I (No. 40) = 11 years; *ṭuppišu* kings 42-47 = 0 years; kings 61, 79, 82, and 83 = higher variants (following BRINKMAN 1977); kings 65 + 66 = 29 years; *ṭuppišu* kings 84 + 85 = 0 years; [*14**] = reconstructed regnal period.

Base Chronology Corrected against Solar Dates (–18 years)

87.	Tiglath-pileser I	1114-1076	(39)		
86.	Aššur-rēša-iši I	1132-1115	(18)		
85.	Mutakkil-Nusku	1133	*ṭuppišu*		
84.	Ninurta-tukulti-Aššur	1133	*ṭuppišu*		
*83.	Aššur-dān I	1177-1133	(45)		–1 year
*82.	Ninurta-apil-Ekur	1189-1178	(12)		–1 year
81.	Enlil-kudurrī-uṣur	1194-1190	(5)		
80.	Aššur-nīrārī III	1200-1195	(6)		
79.	Aššur-nādin-apli	1204-1201	(4)		
*78.	Tukulti-Ninurta I	1240-1205	(36)		–1 year
*77.	Shalmaneser I	1269-1241	(29)		–1 year
*76.	Adad-nīrārī I	1300-1270	(31)		–1 year
*75.	Arik-dēn-ili	1311-1301	(11)		–1 year
74.	Enlil-nīrārī	1321-1312	(10)		
*73.	Aššur-uballiṭ I	1356-1322	(35)		–1 year
*72.	Erība-Adad I	1383-1357	(27)		
71.	Aššur-nādin-aḫḫē II	1393-1384	(10)		
70.	Aššur-rē'im-nišēšu	1401-1394	(8)		
*69.	Aššur-bēl-nišēšu	1409-1402	(8)		–1 year
68.	Aššur-nīrārī II	1416-1410	(7)		
67.	Enlil-nāṣir II	1422-1417	(6)		
*66.	Aššur-nādin-aḫḫē I	*1436-1423*	[*14**]		–1 year
65.	Aššur-rabi I	*1450-1437*	[*14**]		
64.	Aššur-šadûni	1450	(1 mo.)		
63.	Nūr-ili	1462-1451	(12)		
*62.	Enlil-nāṣir I	1474-1463	(12)		–1 year
61.	Puzur-Aššur III	1498-1475	(24)		
*60.	Aššur-nīrārī I	1523-1499	(25)		–1 year
*59.	Šamšī-Adad III	1538-1524	(15)		–1 year
58.	Išme-Dagan II	1554-1539	(16)		
57.	Šamšī-Adad II	1560-1555	(6)		
*56.	Ērišu III	1572-1561	(12)		–1 year
55.	Šarma-Adad II	1575-1573	(3)		
54.	Šū-Ninūa	1589-1576	(14)		
53.	Lullaya	1595-1590	(6)		
*52.	Bazaya	1622-1596	(27)		–1 year
*51.	IB.TAR-Sîn	1633-1623	(11)		–1 year
50.	Šarma-Adad I	1645-1634	(12)		
*49.	Libbaya	1661-1646	(16)		–1 year
48.	Bēlu-bāni	1671-1662	(10)		
47.	Adasi	*1672*	*bāb ṭuppišu*		
46.	Adad-ṣalūlu	*1672*	*bāb ṭuppišu*		
45.	Ipqi-Ištar	*1672*	*bāb ṭuppišu*		
44.	Sîn-namir	*1672*	*bāb ṭuppišu*		
43.	Nāṣir-Sîn	*1672*	*bāb ṭuppišu*	41c. Asīnum	
42.	Aššur-apla-idi	*1672*	*bāb ṭuppišu*	41b. Rimu-x	
41.	Aššur-dugul	1677-1672	(6)	41a. Mut-Aškur	
*40.	Išme-Dagan I	1687-1678	(10)		–1 year
*39.	Šamšī-Adad I	**1719-1688**	(32)		–1 year

On the premise that the lunar calendar was used in Assyria until the reign of Tiglath-pileser I (1114-1076), a reduction of 1 year every 33 years (or 3 years per century) is made in the base chronology computed above (* marks a reign in which 1 year has been subtracted).

3.3.3. Lower Assyrian Kinglist Variants

According to the procedure set forth above in Section 3.1.3 for treating the kinglist variants, the following reductions in our corrected base chronology are also deemed possible :

–10 years	(if we employ the variants in the Nassouhi list) ;
–11 years	(if we use the variants attested in the SDAS list or restore the regnal period of No. 61 in the Khorsabad list as "24") ; and
–21 years	(if we use a combination of the lowest possible variants from the lists or restore the regnal period of No. 61 in the Khorsabad list as "14").

When these reductions are made, we arrive at the following range of dates for the reign of Šamšī-Adad I :[264]

Chron. 1	1719-1688 BC	(corrected base chronology),
Chron. 2	1709-1678 BC	(–10 years),
Chron. 3	1708-1677 BC	(–11 years),
Chron. 4	1698-1667 BC	(–21 years).

3.3.4. Impact of the Lower Dates of Šamšī-Adad on the Date of Hammurabi Year 1 and Samsuditana Year 31 (= the Supposed Date of the Fall of Babylon)

Šamšī-Adad died in Hammurabi year 12, 13, or 17.[265] This information (regardless of which of the three dates we accept) provides the crucial link between the Assyrian and Babylonian chronological sequences for the two-century period preceding the fall of Babylon, an event that is thought to have occurred in Samsuditana year 31 (= 1595 BC, Middle Chronology). Assuming that Samsuditana's reign was not longer than 31 years (and Ammiṣaduqa's was 21 years),[266] the interval separating Hammurabi year 1 and Samsuditana year 31 was 197 years. Knowing this we can calculate a range of dates for the fall of Babylon based on our (lower) computations of the range of dates for Šamšī-Adad. All we need to do is establish the possibilities for Hammurabi year 1 and subtract 197 years from them. The possibilities for Hammurabi year 1 and, consequently, of Samsuditana year 31, would then be [267]

---

264 A more precise date for Šamšī-Adad's reign will be suggested in Chapter 5, after the presentation of the astronomical evidence.

265 CHARPIN and DURAND 1985, 306-308 ; VEENHOF 1985, 217-218 ; but cf. WHITING 1990. See n. 231 above.

266 The precise lengths of both reigns remain uncertain. "31" and "21" are the respective figures cited in Kinglist B, a source that elsewhere exhibits numerous errors. On the length of Samsuditana's reign specifically, see FEIGIN and LANDSBERGER 1955, 159.

267 The following calculations consider only the dates placing the death of Šamšī-Adad in the years Hammurabi 12 and 17.

	Death of Š-A = Hammurabi 12		*Death of Š-A = Hammurabi 17*	
	Ha 1	Sd 31	Ha 1	Sd 31
Chron. 1 (Š-A = 1719-1688)	1699 (-197 =)	1502	1704 (-197 =)	1507 [268]
Chron. 2 (Š-A = 1709-1678)	1689 (-197 =)	1492	1694 (-197 =)	1497
Chron. 3 (Š-A = 1708-1677)	1688 (-197 =)	1491	1693 (-197 =)	1496
Chron. 4 (Š-A = 1698-1667)	1678 (-197 =)	1481	1683 (-197 =)	1486

The last set of dates, based on Chron. 4, are probably too low, however. This assessment is based on the following reasoning :

(1) We have accepted the use in Assyria of a lunar calendar without intercalary months before the reign of Tiglath-pileser I and have therefore subtracted 3 years per century from the Assyrian sequence before 1114. Because Babylonian chronology is based on this sequence, a reduction of about 5 years is required in the most commonly cited regnal dates of the Kassite rulers.[269]

(2) Because adjustments in Babylonian chronology also affect Egyptian chronology (due to Amarna-Period synchronisms), the reduction of an additional 11 years in Kassite-Period dates required by our Chron. 4 [270] would necessitate that we also lower New Kingdom dates by a corresponding number of years or more,[271] resulting in an ultra-low Egyptian chronology. Such a scheme of reckoning presently has few advocates. A reduction of some 5-6 years, however, would fit the widely accepted "low chronology" (which sets the accession year of Ramses II in 1279 BC).

(3) Therefore, we posit that the most likely range of dates for the fall of Babylon is 1507-1491 BC (judging 1486 and 1481 to be too low).

A table of the key synchronisms linking the Assyrian, Babylonian, and Egyptian sequences is presented below. The Assyrian dates are cited according to our corrected base chronology. The Babylonian dates are all 5 years lower than those reconstructed by BRINKMAN (1976, 31). Finally, the Egyptian dates are calculated on the assumption that the accession year of Ramses II was 1279 BC. (We have also included the synchronism between Ulam-Buriaš, son of Burna-Buriaš, and Ea-gamil, king of the Sealand, because we will refer to it later.)

---

268 It should be noted that WEIDNER (1945-51, 91) also computed Hammurabi year 1 to be 1704. DE LIAGRE BÖHL (1946, 352) had earlier arrived at the same figure. Compare also the chronology of SCHUBERT (1948, 33), who set Samsuditana year 31 at 1507 (on the basis of Weidner's calculations [1948, 28-29]).

269 For the approximate 5-year downward adjustment necessitated by the correction of Assyrian lunar dates to solar dates (and a resulting variation of ± 7 years), see BRINKMAN 1976, 32, n. 89. The most commonly cited Kassite dates are those calculated by BRINKMAN 1976, 31.

270 The 11-year reduction is predicated upon acceptance of a 3-year reign (instead of 13) for the Assyrian king Ninurta-apil-Ekur (No. 82) and a 3-year reign (instead of 4) for Aššur-nādin-apli (No. 79).

271 VON BECKERATH 1992. All New Kingdom regnal dates after those of Ahmose are ultimately anchored by the apparent reference in Papyrus Ebers to an observation of the heliacal rising of Sirius during the ninth year of Amenophis I, allowing the calculation of the beginning of a Sothic period (see, for example, GRIMAL 1992, 202). The anchor in question, however, can be placed either in 1537 or in 1517 BC, depending on whether the observation giving rise to it was made in Memphis or in Thebes (GRIMAL 1992, 51, 202). But see now VON BECKERATH 1997, 46, 50 ; we thank B. Hrouda for having drawn our attention to this new publication, which, however, appeared during final proof corrections.

Synchronisms Linking the Assyrian, Babylonian, and Egyptian Sequences

Assyria			*Babylonia*				*Egypt*	
87. Tiglath-pileser I	1114-1076							
86. Aššur-rēša-iši I	1132-1115							
85. Mutakkil-Nusku	1133							
84. Ninurta-tukulti-Aššur	1133							
83. Aššur-dān I	**1177-1133**	⇨	**35. Zababa-šuma-iddina**	**1153**				
			34. Marduk-apla-iddina I	1166-1154				
			33. Meli-Šipak	1181-1167				
82. Ninurta-apil-Ekur	**1189-1178**	⇨	**Adad-šuma-uṣur**					
81. Enlil-kudurrī-uṣur	**1194-1190**	⇨	**Adad-šuma-uṣur**					
80. Aššur-nīrārī III	**1200-1195**	⇨	**Adad-šuma-uṣur**					
79. Aššur-nādin-apli	1204-1201		"					
Tukulti-Ninurta I		⇨	**32. Adad-šuma-uṣur**	**1211-1182**				
"			31. Adad-šuma-iddina	1217-1212				
"			30. Kadašman-Ḫarbe II	1218				
"			29. Enlil-nādin-šumi	1219				
Tukulti-Ninurta I		=	**28a. Tukulti-Ninurta I**	**1220**				
78. Tukulti-Ninurta I	**1240-1205**	⇨	**28. Kaštiliašu IV**	**1227-1220**				
			27. Šagarakti-Šuriaš	1240-1228				
			26. Kudur-Enlil	1249-1241				
77. Shalmaneser I	1269-1241		25. Kadašman-Enlil II	1258-1250				
Adad-nīrārī I		⇨	**24. Kadašman-Turgu**	**1276-1259**				
76. Adad-nīrārī I	**1300-1270**	⇨	**23. Nazi-Maruttaš**	**1302-1277**				
75. Arik-dēn-ili	1311-1301							
74. Enlil-nīrārī	**1321-1312**	⇨	**Kurigalzu II**					
Aššur-uballiṭ I		⇨	**22. Kurigalzu II**	**1327-1303**				
Aššur-uballiṭ I		⇨	**21. Nazi-Bugaš**	**1328**				
Aššur-uballiṭ I		⇨	**20. Kara-ḫardaš**	**1328**		⇨	**Tutankhamun** [272]	**1333-1323**
73. Aššur-uballiṭ I	**1356-1322**	⇨	**19. Burna-Buriaš II**	**1354-1328**	⇨ ⇗ ⇘	⇨	**Akhenaton**	**1351-1334**
72. Erība-Adad I	1383-1357		**18. Kadašman-Enlil I**	**(1369)-1355**	⇨	⇨	**Amenophis III**	**1388-1351/50**
71. Aššur-nādin-aḫḫē II	1393-1384							
70. Aššur-rē'im-nišēšu	1401-1394		17. Kurigalzu I					
			16. Kadašman-Ḫarbe I					
69. Aššur-bēl-nišēšu	**1409-1402**	⇨	**15. Kara-indaš**					
68. Aššur-nīrārī II	1416-1410							
67. Enlil-nāṣir II	1422-1417							
66. Aššur-nādin-aḫḫē I	[*1436-1423*]							
65. Aššur-rabi I	[*1450-1437*]						*Sealand*	
64. Aššur-šadûni	1450		Agum					
63. Nūr-ili	1462-1451		**Ulam-Buriaš**		⇨		**Ea-gamil**	
62. Enlil-nāṣir I	1474-1463							
61. Puzur-Aššur III	**1498-1475**	⇨	**10. Burna-Buriaš I**					

Tukulti-Ninurta ⇨ **Kaštiliašu IV** = synchronism

[272] The dates of Tutankhamun, Akhenaton, and Amenophis III follow those proposed by VON BECKERATH 1997, 190.

3.3.5. Implications for the Interpretation of Babylonian Kinglist A

Our argument to shorten Mesopotamian chronology in the second millennium by a magnitude of 85-105 years implies that we must reject the testimony of Kinglist A regarding the length of the First Dynasty of the Sealand. The kinglist states that the length of this dynasty was 368 years.[273] However, we know that the first king of the dynasty, Iluma-AN, was a contemporary of Samsuiluna, and that Ea-gamil, the last king, was a contemporary of Ulam-Buriaš, the brother of Kaštiliaš.[274] If this Kaštiliaš is placed after Burna-Buriaš I (No. 10) in the Kassite sequence (which is the most reasonable fit),[275] only about 200 years separated Iluma-AN and Ea-gamil ; and therefore the figure is erroneous.[276]

The length of the Kassite Dynasty cited in Kinglist A — 576 years — is also dubious, since, according to our proposed shortened chronology, the beginning of the dynasty would have to be placed some 75-95 years before the time of Samsuiluna and Rīm-Sîn II, when Old Babylonian year names first mention Kassites.[277]

Since forty percent of the royal names in Kinglist A appear in truncated form, and many of these abbreviations occur in groups, the text in its present form can be understood to have derived from a source that was damaged already in antiquity.[278] The totals in question, therefore, are perhaps reconstructions.

3.3.6. Summary of the Argument from Chronological Sources

In this chapter, we have presented an argument that the principal Mesopotamian textual sources used to reconstruct the chronology of the second millennium admit the possibility of a chronology that is some 85-105 years lower than the one now most commonly accepted (the so-called Middle Chronology). Our analysis focused primarily on the Assyrian Kinglist tradition (AKL), inasmuch as almost all Mesopotamian dates — especially for the period in question — are calculated either directly or indirectly on the basis of the data contained therein.

We first adopted a set of premises upon which our analysis would be based. The following positions were adopted :[279] (1) the Assyrian calendar was based on the lunar year, without intercalary

---

273 GRAYSON 1980-83, 91.

274 GRAYSON 1975, 156 (Chronicle of Early Kings).

275 BRINKMAN 1976, 12.

276 BRINKMAN (1977, 346, n. 5) noted already that the figures given in Kinglist A for the lengths of reign of this dynasty are difficult to place in any coherent chronology and that some of the numbers, especially the longer reigns, should possibly be reduced.

277 BRINKMAN 1976, 32, and n. 88. One should note that one of the factors said to have caused the author the most uneasiness over his reconstruction of the dates for the earliest Kassite kings on the basis of the total for the dynasty given in Kinglist A was "the necessity of spreading kings 4-14 over such a long period of time" (1976, 33, n. 92). He notes elsewhere that the figures for the lengths of reign that he has reconstructed partly on the basis of this data "have several obvious difficulties, not the least of which is that half the kings of the dynasty (Nos. ?19-36) would account for only 35.65% of the total number of years" (1976, 27).

278 Compare also BRINKMAN 1976, 426-427.

279 For the arguments, see Sections 3.1.2 and 3.1.3 above.

months, before the reign of Tiglath-pileser I, allowing a reduction of 3 years per century prior to 1114 BC ; (2) the reign of Išme-Dagan I, son of Šamšī-Adad I, lasted 11 years instead of 40 years assigned to him in the AKL, allowing a reduction of 29 years ; (3) the word *ṭuppišu*, used in the AKL to describe several kings' reigns, represents "0 years" in terms of chronological reckoning ; and (4) the combined reigns of kings Aššur-rabi I (65) and Aššur-nādin-aḫḫē I (66), whose regnal periods are missing in the AKL, was 29 years.[280]

We next examined the inscriptions of Assyrian kings that contain statements concerning successive rebuildings of the Aššur and Anu-Adad temples in Assur (*Distanzangaben*) to determine if the range of dates they yield for the building activities of Šamšī-Adad I is sufficiently narrow to serve as a basis for reconstructing not only the pre-1500 chronology of Assyria but also that of Babylonia during the same period, since the latter hinges upon an important synchronism between Šamšī-Adad I and Hammurabi of Babylon. These statements were shown to contradict one another and therefore offer almost no help in establishing dates for the reign of Šamšī-Adad.

We then turned to an analysis of our most important source, the Assyrian Kinglist. Based on the premises outlined above, we arrived first at a base chronology, by means of dead reckoning, which placed the reign of Šamšī-Adad I in 1737-1705 BC. Next, on the premise that the lunar calendar was used in Assyria before the reign of Tiglath-pileser I (1114-1076), we made a reduction in the base chronology of 1 year every 33 years (or 3 years per century = –18), resulting in regnal dates of 1719-1688 BC for this king. Then, according to the procedure set forth in Section 3.1.3 for treating kinglist variants, we subtracted 10, 11, and 21 years from the last-mentioned dates and arrived at, respectively, 1709-1678, 1708-1677, and 1698-1667 as other possible dates for the reign of Šamšī-Adad I.

Finally, we turned to the question of the date of the fall of Babylon, which is thought to have occurred in Samsuditana year 31.[281] Based on the synchronism placing the death of Šamšī-Adad I in year 12, 13, or 17 of Hammurabi, we established four possible dates for Hammurabi year 1 based on the four sets of dates for the reign of Šamšī-Adad mentioned in the preceding paragraph. Because 197 years separated Hammurabi year 1 and Samsuditana year 31, we calculated a range of dates that placed the fall of Babylon (= Samsuditana 31) sometime between 1507 and 1481. The final set of dates calculated on this basis — 1486 and 1481 — was thought to be too low because of potential conflicts with Amarna-Period synchronisms.[282] Therefore, we ultimately arrived at 1507-1491 as the most likely period in which to place the fall of Babylon.

It should be stressed that this range of dates is only an approximation. While the textual sources we have examined, including the various manuscripts of the Assyrian Kinglist, permit us to construct a plausible lower chronology that is consistent with our interpretation of the archaeological evidence, they do not allow us to calculate anything resembling an absolute date for the fall of Babylon. How, then, can we arrive at a more precise date for this pivotal event ?

---

280 It is unlikely that this figure should be higher ; see Section 3.2 above.

281 See n. 266 above.

282 See p. 65.

3.4. Ancient Lunar Eclipse Data

The Babylonian series of celestial omens called *Enūma Anu Enlil*, which is comprised of about seventy tablets, contains not only the "Venus Tablet" (which links Ammiṣaduqa year 8 with a recurring Venus phenomenon), but also detailed descriptions of lunar-eclipse observations. Because two of these observations are linked with well-known historical events of the Ur III Period, we should be able to use them to fix, in absolute time, both the eclipses that they describe and the ancient events with which they are associated. The potential importance of celestial observations linked with historical events for the reckoning of absolute chronology is self-evident. We therefore now turn to an astronomical analysis of both the Venus Tablet and the pertinent sections of *Enūma Anu Enlil* containing the eclipse observations we have just mentioned.

4.

The Astronomical Data

Introduction

V.G. Gurzadyan has examined two sets of ancient astronomical data in order to determine their usefulness in helping to establish an absolute Mesopotamian chronology for the second millennium BC :

a) information concerning the first and the last visibilities of Venus recorded in the so-called "Venus Tablet of Ammiṣaduqa" ;[283] and

b) two lunar eclipses mentioned in *Enūma Anu Enlil* Tablets 20 and 21.[284]

The results of the examination of this material are discussed in this chapter.

Gurzadyan has also identified possible candidates for a lunar eclipse mentioned in two texts excavated at Tell Muḫammad, a site near Tell Harmal in Baghdad. Information about this eclipse and its wider chronological significance will be presented below in Chapter 5.

Before turning to the discussion of the "Venus Tablet" and the lunar eclipses of *Enūma Anu Enlil*, we should briefly review the basics of Babylonian astronomical methodology. In contrast with the Ptolemaic system, the Babylonian system is purely positional. Although sequences of astronomical events — lunar phases, eclipses, stationary points, and the first and last appearances of planets — were recorded, no attempt was made to explain the apparent motion of the celestial bodies involved. The observed periodicity or semiperiodicity of certain sequences was itself sufficient for the prediction of future events. In practice, when a long sequence was involved — for example, the 19-year calendric cycle, which consisted of 12 years of 12 lunar months each and 7 years of 13 lunar months each — the need for accurate observational data was secondary to the need to account for the entire period under consideration. As a result, the tabulated numbers in the astronomical texts do not always represent a sequence of real events. In other words, the "observations" recorded in these texts are not necessarily true observations at all, but rather just the numbers that were required to fit the cycle.[285] It is not impossible that such methods were utilized by Ptolemy as well.[286]

---

283 Reiner and Pingree 1975.

284 Weidner 1954-56 ; Rochberg-Halton 1988.

285 Neugebauer 1967 ; 1975, 354-363 ; 1983a, 18-19.

286 Newton 1976 ; 1977.

As for the fundamental accuracy of the data, even the positional information in the tablets cannot be traced with absolute confidence. For example, the horizontal coordinates are off by more than 45 degrees in one-sixth of the observations. Even for the late periods no evidence exists that would permit the secure matching of the Babylonian coordinates with modern ones.[287]

Therefore, because of interpretational, methodological, and terminological uncertainties, the information recovered from such texts is ambiguous. In the case of the Venus Tablet, the later sections are also clearly corrupted and distorted. The data of this tablet will therefore remain problematic until new evidence is brought to light. The problems involving the motion of celestial bodies, however, do not apply to the eclipse observations.

4.1. THE "VENUS TABLET OF AMMIṢADUQA"

The so-called Venus Tablet, which is incorporated in the astrological series known as *Enūma Anu Enlil*, contains information on the first and the last visibilities of Venus during a 21-year period that has been assumed to correspond with the reign of Ammiṣaduqa. The data in this text are incomplete and frequently distorted, and opinions have differed over the text's usefulness in providing a basis for second-millennium chronology. Thus, REINER and PINGREE (1975) seem to believe that it is difficult to extract reliable data from the later portions of the tablet,[288] while Huber asserts that through statistical methods a trustworthy "signal" can be discerned in the "noise" of incompleteness and distortion.[289]

The analysis undertaken by HUBER (1987b) led him to the conclusion that the High Chronology (Ammiṣaduqa year 1 = -1701 [290] [1702 BC]) best fits the data. He concluded that the Middle Chronology (Aṣ 1 = -1645 [1646 BC]) produces the poorest match, while the Low Chronology is somewhere between the previous two (Aṣ 1 = -1581 [1582 BC]). Huber's analysis is biased principally by the *a priori* assumption that at least one of these three chronologies is correct. However, because the observational data on Venus also depends on local conditions, the 8-year cycle, in the absence of this information, is the only reliable data that can be extracted from the Venus Tablet. In other words, the 56/64-year cycle upon which the High-Middle-Low scheme of chronological reckoning is based is not necessarily established on the basis of the evidence presently found in this text.

To avoid misinterpretation and erroneous evaluation of the information contained in the Venus Tablet, we must first know what characteristics to expect in Babylonian astronomical records.

The periodicity of Venus — 5 synodic periods = 8 sidereal years — is in reality only approximate because the Venus/Earth resonances yield :

$$\omega_V / \omega_E = 1152/720$$

---

287 See HUBER 1987b.

288 In their words : "That the majority of the dates of the first 8-year cycle and the beginning of the second form a valid negative argument for establishing the date of the beginning of Ammiṣaduqa's reign seems to us to be admissible. We do not see the absolute necessity of accepting the hypothesis that the dates preserved in the rest of the text must also belong to Ammiṣaduqa's reign" (REINER and PINGREE 1975, 25).

289 HUBER *et al.* 1982 ; HUBER 1987a ; 1987b.

290 -1701 takes in account that there is no year 0.

The corresponding difference in -2.30 *mod*60° leads to a -4.10 day shift in the 8-sidereal-year period. This is termed System A_1 by NEUGEBAUER (1975, 463). However, Babylonian astronomers also employed a second system, System A_2, (*ibid.*) which assumes a -2.40 change in the longitudes and a -4 day shift for the period.

Thus, one encounters the situation where in a single astronomical text [291] the phases ψ, Ω, and ϕ fit System A_1, while the coordinates of the first and last appearances of Venus Γ and Σ are presented according to System A_2. As a result, an inevitable distortion will appear in the data, and any probability analysis using ephemerides tables will be meaningless. This corroborates the view that one should not expect all tabulated data in Babylonian astronomical records necessarily to represent real observational events, and that it is not justifiable to draw chronological conclusions from such data (VAN DER WARDEN 1957).

In view of these difficulties, one cannot expect to obtain unbiased statistical information from the Venus Tablet data. To check this, we first calculated the parameters of the first and last visibilities of Venus corresponding to the year we will propose in Chapter 5 for the beginning of Ammiṣaduqa year 1, -1549 (1550 BC), by means of the integration of the orbits.[292] We then carried out a statistical analysis of the early and late departures from the calculated coordinates of the appearances, both for the High, Middle, and Low Chronology dates for Ammiṣaduqa year 1 (-1701, -1645, and -1581) and then for our Ammiṣaduqa year 1 (-1549). The following table represents the results for the *average deviation* (*a*), the *standard deviation* (σ), the *variance* (*var*), and *the 3rd moment* (*s*) :

$$s = 1/N \sum (x_j - \bar{x})^3 / \sigma^3 ;$$

also *the 4th moment* (*k*) :

$$k = 1/N \sum (x_j - \bar{x})^4 / \sigma^4 - 3.$$

Statistics of the Late Departures of Venus [293]

Ammiṣaduqa year 1 =	-1701	-1645	-1581	-1549
a	2.0	1.2	1.25	2.0
σ	2.64	1.73	1.73	2.42
var	7.0	3.0	3.0	6.0
s	-0.32	-0.57	-0.65	-0.22
k	-2.0	-1.77	-1.74	-2.28

291 NEUGEBAUER 1983b, No. 420 + 821b.

292 For the method, see NEWHALL *et al.* 1983, 150 ; and LASKAR 1994, 183.

293 Only the results for the late departures are given here ; but the situation is similar for the early departures.

It is readily apparent from the above tabulations that the statistical analysis does not indicate any preference for the High Chronology, thus demonstrating that we are dealing with absolutely noisy data, from which we cannot reach any reliable conclusions.

4.2. THE UR III LUNAR ECLIPSES

Enūma Anu Enlil Tablet 20 [294] describes a lunar eclipse that is associated with the death of an Ur III king (almost certainly to be identified as Šulgi) and the succession of his son (understood to be Amar-Sîn).[295] According to the text, the eclipse was observed in the month *Simānu* (May-June), day 14, beginning in the first watch of the night. It began on the "upper" [296] east side and cleared the moon on the "lower" west side.

Enūma Anu Enlil Tablet 21 describes an eclipse that was observed in the month of *Addaru* (February-March), also on day 14.[297] It is believed to be associated with Ibbi-Sîn's penultimate or final year, inasmuch as it predicts the fall of Ur.[298] This eclipse began on the south side of the moon during the first watch.

The eclipses are described in considerable detail. The day of the month is given — in both cases the 14th — along with the specific watch of the night in which each began. The direction of each eclipse is also described. Therefore, since it is known that 41-44 years separated the two events,[299] it would seem to be a straightforward matter to identify the eclipses in question. However, as has already been observed by ROCHBERG-HALTON (1988), the 14th day of the month is the most probable day of lunar eclipses and, therefore, cannot be taken seriously into account. Therefore, the description of the direction of the eclipses and the description of the watch period in which they began seem to be our most reliable data.

Assuming that the so-called High Chronology is correct (Ammiṣaduqa year 1 beginning in -1701 [1702 BC]), HUBER (1987a) dated the two Ur lunar eclipses as follows :

> -2094 (2095 BC), July 25 : total eclipse (occultation 1.32 [300]) ; started on the east-north (103) at 19.54 and reached totality at 20.77 [301] (corresponds with the eclipse mentioned in *Enūma Anu Enlil* Tablet 20) ;

---

294 ROCHBERG-HALTON 1988, 189-192.

295 See Section 5.1.

296 In this context, "upper" means "above the horizon" ; it does not indicate a geographical direction. Therefore, this detail is of no help for the characterization of the eclipse (if it began on the "lower" east [= "below the horizon"] the eclipse could not, of course, have been observed).

297 Both eclipses are said to have occurred the 14th day of the month, which is the most probable day of a lunar eclipse.

298 ROCHBERG-HALTON 1988, 248.

299 We assume that the aforementioned eclipse descriptions in *Enūma Anu Enlil* refer to real lunar eclipses that happened shortly before the events they predict — that is, we assume that they took place either in the last or next-to-last years of the reigns of Šulgi and Ibbi-Sîn, respectively. Therefore, 41 years, 42 years, 43 years, and 44 years represent the possible intervals between the penultimate or final year of Šulgi and the penultimate or final year of Ibbi-Sîn, the last king of the Ur III Dynasty, depending on whether the latter's reign was 24 or 25 years (Middle Chronology : 2048/47-2006/05/04 BC).

300 An occultation of over 1.0 is a total eclipse.

301 HUBER 1987a, table 1.

-2052 (2053 BC), April 13 : partial eclipse (maximum occultation 0.6) ; started on the south-east at 21.34 (corresponds with the eclipse mentioned in *Enūma Anu Enlil* Tablet 21).

Huber considers these two eclipses as a crucial supporting argument for his adoption of the High Chronology on the basis of the Venus Tablet. However, as has already been mentioned, eclipses are comparatively common occurrences, so if one wants to make use of eclipse data, one must first determine the time-span in which to look for them. Huber, for example, chose only the three principal Venus chronologies.

In the present study, archaeological and historical arguments have been used to conclude that the correct chronology is, at the very least, shorter than the Middle Chronology. Since the Venus data may be too problematical to use, we have also turned to the data of the Ur III eclipses to see if they support a shorter chronology.

We scanned not only the 150-year period before the traditional Middle Chronology date for the fall of Ur — which, according to the date list set forth by J.A. Brinkman,[302] would have taken place in either -2004 (2005 BC) or -2003 (2004 BC) — but also the 150-year period afterwards ; in other words, we examined a 300-year period between -2150 and -1850, inclusive. Our aim was to locate, in terms of absolute chronology, an eclipse that matched the description of the one predicting the fall of Ur found in *Enūma Anu Enlil* Tablet 21, and that could also be placed 41 to 44 years after an eclipse matching the description of the one predicting the death of Šulgi found in *Enūma Anu Enlil* Tablet 20. Only two of the eclipses that could have been observed in Babylonia during this 300-year period were found to accord with the observations preserved in *Enūma Anu Enlil* :

-1953 [303] (1954 BC) June 27 : total eclipse (occultation 1.4) ; started on the east (77,3) at 18.10 (and ended at 20.06) ;

-1911 (1912 BC) March 16 : partial eclipse (maximum occultation 0.6) ; started on the south (339) at 18.09 (and ended at 21.07).

It will be observed that these two eclipses not only perfectly satisfy the condition of the "first watch" (18.00-22.00) specified in the Simānu and Addaru eclipses of *Enūma Anu Enlil* Tablets 20 and 21, but they also perfectly fit the information concerning their direction.[304] Huber's two eclipses of -2094 and -2052, by contrast, cannot be decisive in supporting the High Chronology, since the two eclipses of -1953 and -1911 fit the ancient descriptions at a higher confidence level. Moreover, Huber's estimations of statistical significance seem to be somewhat simplified. Along with simple combinatorics one also has to estimate the contribution of distortion in the identification of eclipses that are determined by too many free parameters.

---

302 BRINKMAN 1977, 336, and 346, n. 3.

303 We assume that the change of the rotation period of the Earth due to lunar and solar tides — about 2 milliseconds/century — as well as lunar deceleration — 26 arcsec/(century)^2 — which are shown to be adequate at least up to 700 BC (STEPHENSON and SAID 1989 ; STEPHENSON and YAU 1992 ; STEPHENSON 1996) remain valid also to 2000 BC.

304 These descriptions in *Enūma Anu Enlil* fit better with the modern reconstructions than do some of those recorded by Ptolemy (from Babylonian evidence) for the first millennium BC (see TOOMER 1984, 191-192 [Merodach-baladan II eclipses] and 253-254 [Cambyses eclipse]). For various reasons not all the astronomical data quoted by Ptolemy are accurate (see NEWTON 1976). For example, the description of the Cambyses eclipse in STRASSMAIER 1890, No. 40, l. 45-46 fits the modern reconstruction better than does the Ptolemaic text.

4.3. SUMMARY

The analysis above enables us to draw the following conclusions :

1. Because of distortions in the Venus Tablet data we cannot draw from them any statistically significant unbiased conclusions that would allow us to choose one particular chronological scheme over another. Moreover, the recognizable features of similar Babylonian tabular astronomical information indicate that numerical evaluations of confidence levels for the various possible chronological systems derived from the Venus Tablet data are not justified. The only reliable information extractable from the Venus Tablet is the condition that Ammiṣaduqa's first regnal year must be identified with a year in which the Venus phenomenon (recurring every eight years) took place.
2. The data from *Enūma Anu Enlil* Tablets 20 and 21, describing two eclipses connected with historical events of the Ur III Period, though incomplete, contain sufficient information to identify them with the two eclipses of -1953 and -1911. These eclipses, 141 years later than those proposed by Huber, fit the time-range suggested by the archaeological and historical information we have adduced to show that the correct chronology is, at the very least, lower than the Middle Chronology. They also fit the ancient eclipse descriptions at a higher level of confidence than those that have been put forward to substantiate the High Chronology.

With this information — the eight-year cycle of Venus and the absolute dates of the two Ur III eclipses — we can fix the date of Ammiṣaduqa's first year of reign and, by extension, the date of the fall of Babylon. It is to these tasks that we now turn in Chapter 5.

5.

THE FALL OF BABYLON AND ITS RESETTLEMENT

A detailed study of the most frequently produced forms of the second-millennium Babylonian pottery corpus shows that the formal similarities of the shapes produced just before the end of the First Dynasty of Babylon [305] and those produced slightly before 1400 BC cannot be separated in time by two hundred years or more.[306] In other words, very convincing archaeological evidence shows that the Middle Chronology is too high.

However, the two pottery sequences considered here — the Old Babylonian and the Kassite — cannot be linked together in any excavated sequence located between the Tigris and the Euphrates in southern Mesopotamia, because the sites that have been dug in this region all appear to have been deurbanized, a process that began about 140 years before the end of the First Dynasty of Babylon and culminated with the fall of the capital. Our investigation, therefore, turned to an analysis of the stratigraphical sequences and associated pottery found at different excavations located on the periphery of Babylonia. Presently only one site has provided significant published material remains that can be attributed to the period between the fall of Babylon and the time around 1400 BC : Susa. A second site — Tell Muḫammad located in Baghdad, near Tell Harmal, and dug by Iraqi teams — has also yielded material from this period, but it has not yet been published.[307]

This excursion into outlying areas (as seen from the Babylonian heartland) has enabled us to reconstruct the entire evolution of the principal pottery shapes produced between the end of the First Dynasty of Babylon and the time around 1400 BC. The dynamic of this formal evolution suggests a shortening of the Middle Chronology by about 100 years.

The chronological sources — especially the Assyrian Kinglist tradition — also indicate that it is possible to shorten the Middle Chronology. A reduction on the order of 85-105 years has been posited. We began by calculating the possible dates for Šamšī-Adad's rebuilding of the Aššur and Anu-Adad temples based on data found in the inscriptions of Shalmaneser I, Tiglath-pileser I, and Esarhaddon. This evidence was found to be internally inconsistent and to yield a range of dates too wide to be of use in reconstructing the chronology of the second millennium. We therefore turned to the kinglist data, which, although fraught with interpretational difficulties, remain the most reliable

[305] Revealed only recently by excavations conducted at Tell ed-Dēr (Sippar-Amnānum), Tell ed-Deylam (Dilbat), and Khirbet ed-Diniyeh (Ḫarādum).

[306] The evidence of the cylinder seals is consistent with our interpretation of the pottery evidence ; see, in particular, the comments of MATTHEWS (1990, 56-57) and COLLON (1988, 58).

[307] The significance of the texts and other archaeological materials from this site in the present context is discussed below.

chronological source at our disposal. On this basis we were able to narrow the range of Šamšī-Adad's reign to 1719-1667. Finally, because the reign of Šamšī-Adad can be linked directly with that of Hammurabi and the entire Babylonian sequence from the beginning of the Ur III Dynasty to the fall of Babylon, we calculated the latter event to have occurred between 1507 and 1491.[308]

This 16-year span offers more precise chronological brackets than those derived solely from the archaeological evidence lying at the origin of this investigation. In the discussion that follows we will attempt to arrive at a still more precise date for the end of the First Dynasty of Babylon. To accomplish this objective we will begin by examining the results obtained by Gurzadyan in his analysis of two lunar eclipses considered to be directly connected with two historical events of the Ur III Period. These two eclipses will provide the anchor for the absolute chronology that we will propose.

Because the number of years between the fall of Ur and the first regnal year of Ammiṣaduqa is at least approximately known, the following stages of our analysis consist of an attempt to determine, in absolute terms, a) the first year of Ammiṣaduqa's reign (taking into consideration the fact that it has to be fixed within the 8-year cycle of Venus)[309] and b) the final year of the reign of Samsuditana, or in other words, the date of the fall of Babylon. As will become apparent, these two tasks pose problems for which there are not yet ready solutions. A new perspective on the latter problem, however, has been opened up thanks to finds uncovered during the course of excavations at Tell Muḫammad, a site located on the left bank of the Tigris only a few hundred meters from Tell Harmal. Among the most remarkable of these finds is a group of texts dating shortly after the reign of Samsuditana that demonstrate that the Babylonian capital was abandoned for a certain amount of time after the reign of this king. They also yield further astronomical information that can be used to approximate the duration of this abandonment.

5.1. THE ANCHOR FOR AN ABSOLUTE CHRONOLOGY : THE UR III LUNAR ECLIPSES

As we have seen in Chapter 4, Gurzadyan scanned a time-span ranging from 2150 to 1850 BC,[310] attempting to identify 2 lunar eclipses, 41 to 44 years apart, that matched the descriptions of those that were understood to have predicted the death of Šulgi and the fall of Ur.[311] The results — compared with those of HUBER (1987a, table 1) favoring the High Chronology — are recapitulated here :

---

[308] Dates later than 1491 were rejected because of potential conflicts with Babylonian-Egyptian synchronisms after 1400 ; see Section 3.3.4.

[309] As is Aṣ 1 in the High (1702 BC), Middle (1646 BC), and Low Chronology (1582 BC). Consistent with previous studies we introduce into our calculations year 1 of Ammiṣaduqa rather than year 8, the actual date found in the "Venus Tablet."

[310] About 150 years before and 150 years after the traditional Middle Chronology date for the fall of Ur, which, according to the chronological scheme set forth by BRINKMAN (1977, 336 and 346, n. 3), would have taken place in either 2005 or 2004, depending on whether Ibbi-Sin, the last Ur III king, reigned 24 years (Ur-Isin Kinglist ; Sumerian Kinglist mss. WB and J) or 25 years (Sumerian Kinglist mss. P_5 and Su_1) (GRAYSON 1980-83, 90 ; JACOBSEN 1939b, 122-123).

[311] Basing our estimation solely on the evidence of the kinglists, year names, and date lists pertaining to the Ur III Period, we have concluded that 41 to 44 years is the span of time that separated the penultimate year of Šulgi (assuming that the eclipse predicting his death occurred in either his penultimate or final year) and the last year (i.e., either year 24 or 25) of Ibbi-Sîn (assuming that the eclipse predicting the destruction of Ur occurred in his penultimate or final year).

Lunar eclipse predicting the death of a king of Ur (identified as Šulgi) 1)

TEXTUAL EVIDENCE	ASTRONOMICAL RESULTS (Gurzadyan, see Chapter 4)	(HUBER 1987a, table 1)
Šulgi // day 14 // Simānu = **May-June** // year 47/48. Began in the first watch of the night (between 18.00-22.00) ;2) began on the "upper" 3) **east** side.	On -1953, 27 **June** (= 1954 BC) : total eclipse ; started on the **east** at 18.10 (and finished at 20.06).	On -2094, 25 **July** (= 2095 BC) : total eclipse ; started on the **east-north** at 19.54.

1) ROCHBERG-HALTON 1988, 189-192. The eclipse predicts that a son of the king of Ur would wrong his father, that this son would die in the place where the mourning rites of his father were performed, and that a son of the king who was not designated as his father's successor would take the throne. This scenario matches what we know about the circumstances surrounding Šulgi's death and the succession of Amar-Sîn (MICHALOWSKI 1977a ; 1977b).

2) According to the description in Recension A, the eclipse passed the first watch and touched the second (ROCHBERG-HALTON 1988, 190, l. 2). However, according to Recension B, the first watch reached its mid-point (*barārītu imšul*), meaning that the eclipse began and ended before the first watch was half over (ROCHBERG-HALTON 1988, 191, l. 2) ; compare this with Gurzadyan's result.

3) In this context, "upper" means "above the horizon" (see n. 296 above).

Lunar eclipse predicting the destruction of Ur 1)

TEXTUAL EVIDENCE	ASTRONOMICAL RESULTS (Gurzadyan, see Chapter 4)	(HUBER 1987a, table 1)
Ibbi-Sîn // day 14 // Addaru = **February-March** // year 23/24/25. Began in the first watch of the night (between 18.00-22.00) ;2) began on the **south** side.	On -1911, 16 **March** (= 1912 BC) : partial eclipse ; started on the **south** at 18.09 (and finished at 21.07).	On -2052, 13 **April** (= 2053 BC) : partial eclipse ; started on the **south-east** at 21.34.

1) ROCHBERG-HALTON 1988, 248.

2) The eclipse is said to have ended in the morning watch. ROCHBERG-HALTON (1988, 47, and 232, n. 6) judged the duration of the eclipse, as stated in the omen, artificial and astronomically invalid.

The similarities between the information from the textual evidence and Gurzadyan's results are striking,[312] and demonstrate that Huber's dates for the two Ur III eclipses are far from decisive in supporting the High Chronology.

We now have two calculated eclipses, separated by 41 years and 9 months, that are fixed in terms of absolute chronology, and to which we can confidently link two events in historical time — the death of Šulgi and the fall of Ur. According to this information, Šulgi died in 1954 or 1953 BC (depending on whether the eclipse predicting his death occurred in his penultimate or final year), and the fall of Ur occurred some 42 years later, in 1912 or 1911 BC (depending on whether the eclipse predicting the destruction of Ur took place in the dynasty's penultimate or final year).

312 Concerning the 14th day of the month for the occurrence of both eclipses, see p. 74 and n. 297.

5.2. AMMIṢADUQA'S FIRST YEAR OF REIGN

With the date of the fall of Ur fixed, it would seem, at first glance, easy to fix, in absolute terms, the regnal years of the kings of the Isin I, Larsa, and Old Babylonian Dynasties, and, subsequently, the fall of Babylon. This operation, however, requires not only simple arithmetic subtraction but also another chronological anchor, in this case the date of the first year of Ammiṣaduqa's reign. With respect to the astronomical evidence, this year has to be fixed within the 8-year cycle of Venus.[313] In other words, Ammiṣaduqa's first year has to be distant by a multiple of 8 years from, for example, 1646 BC (= Aṣ 1 in the Middle Chronology), which fits the aforementioned cycle.

There are other factors to consider as well. Even a superficial analysis of the chronological data pertaining to the Ur III, Isin I, Larsa, and Old Babylonian Dynasties derived from various kinglists, date lists, compendia of year names, and individual texts and archives reveals the existence of numerous discrepancies in the figures given for individual lengths of reign. Moreover, the prevailing interpretations of the interrelationships among the synchronisms that tie these dynasties together are not ironclad. The following are some of the discrepancies, uncertainties, and problems impeding our ability to reconstruct an accurate relative chronology for the period spanned by these dynasties.

In general we must bear in mind that there are numerous variations in cited lengths of individual reigns between the Larsa Kinglist, the Ur-Isin Kinglist, and the Sumerian Kinglist ;[314] and that the numbers of year names attested for individual reigns during this period often exceed the numbers found on the kinglists — discrepancies that are usually resolved by shoehorning the attested year names into lengths of reigns derived from the kinglists and date lists, which are sometimes based on consensus of opinion rather than on incontrovertible evidence.[315] More specifically : 1) the reign of Amar-Sîn may be 8 years rather than 9 depending on how one interprets the evidence of *ITT* 2/1 907, a text from Umma enclosed in an envelope, in which the inner document is dated to year 8 of Amar-Sîn and the envelope is dated to the first year of the following king, Šū-Sîn ;[316] 2) Ibbi-Sîn is assigned 25 years in two manuscripts of the Sumerian Kinglist but 24 years in two others, as well as in the Ur-Isin Kinglist ;[317] 3) Gungunum has 27 years in the Larsa Kinglist, whereas Sigrist's listing of year names gives him a year 28 ;[318] 4) Rīm-Sîn I is assigned 61 years instead of 60 in the Larsa Kinglist, and we can only guess at the questionable numbers for his six immediate predecessors, including Warad-Sîn, to whom the date list A. 7534 assigns 13 years rather than 12 ;[319] 5) Būr-Sîn reigned 22 years according to the Ur-Isin Kinglist but 21 years according to two manuscripts of the Sumerian Kinglist ;[320] 6) there are other one-year discrepancies between the former and versions of the latter in the numbers attributed to the reigns of Irra-imittī (8 vs. 7), Itēr-piša (3 vs.

313 See Sections 4.1 and 4.3.

314 GRAYSON 1980-83, 89-90, 100 ; JACOBSEN 1939b, 123-127.

315 See, for example, SYKES 1973 ; SIGRIST and GOMI 1991 ; SIGRIST 1988 and 1990.

316 LAFONT 1994, 106-108, 115.

317 JACOBSEN 1939b, 122-123, and n. 331 ; GRAYSON 1980-83, 90.

318 GRAYSON 1980-83, 89 ; SIGRIST 1990, 11.

319 GRAYSON 1980-83, 89 ; STOL 1976, 2-6.

320 GRAYSON 1980-83, 90 ; JACOBSEN 1939b, 126-127.

4), and Urdukuga (also 3 vs. 4);[321] 7) the length of reign of Damiq-ilišu, the final king of the First Dynasty of Isin, is preserved only in the Sumerian Kinglist;[322] and 8) the last rulers of the First Dynasty of Babylon — Ammiṣaduqa and Samsuditana — have their reign-lengths preserved only in Kinglist B, a text that otherwise exhibits many conspicuous errors.[323]

In addition, the most commonly cited interpretations of the interrelationships among the synchronisms that link these dynastic sequences together may have to be revised as more data become available.[324] Particularly vexing is the question of how one matches Ibbi-Sîn year 24 (or 25) with a specific year of Išbi-Erra.

If, however, we accept the results of the well-reasoned analyses of these synchronisms made by Edzard (especially Ibbi-Sîn 24 = Išbi-Irra 13 or 14 [actually 11 + x ≤ 3]) and Stol (Zambīya 2 = Sîn-iqīšam 5 ; Rīm-Sîn I 60 = Hammurabi 30 ; etc.), and if we accept the prevailing consensus of opinion on the numbers of years to be assigned to the Isin I and Larsa Dynasties (224 and 264 years respectively), and to the first 9 kings of the First Dynasty of Babylon (248 years total), then we may conclude that either 359 or 358 years[325] separated the fall of Ur and year 1 of Ammiṣaduqa (the 10th king of the last-named dynasty), depending on whether Ibbi-Sîn, the final Ur III monarch, reigned 25 or 24 years.

If we then subtract 359 and 358 years respectively from 1912 and 1911 BC (the two possible dates for the fall of Ur), we arrive at 1554/53 or 1553/52 BC for Aṣ 1. Unfortunately none of these dates fits within the 8-year cycle of Venus. Two other possibilities, then, have to be considered: 1558 or 1550 BC. If we posit 1558 BC, then only 354 (= 1912 – 1558) or 353 years (= 1911 – 1558) separate the fall of Ur and the advent of Ammiṣaduqa's first regnal year, which would require a shortening by 5 years of the time-span between these two events. This figure seems to be improbable inasmuch as it is already difficult to reconcile all the attested year formulae with the most commonly accepted lengths of reign derived from the date lists and kinglists.[326] More convincing, therefore, would be

1550 BC for the first year of Ammiṣaduqa.

If this date is correct, then 362 or 361 years would separate the two events — 3 years more than are usually assumed. This apparent discrepancy can be partially resolved if we accept the synchronism Ibbi-Sîn 24 = Išbi-Irra 11 and, with it, the order proposed by CRAWFORD (1954) for the first eleven year names of Išbi-Irra.[327] Combining this information with the evidence of

---

321 GRAYSON 1980-83, 90 ; JACOBSEN 1939b, 126-127.

322 JACOBSEN 1939b, 127, n. 363.

323 A date list from the Diyala region preserves 29 (or 30) year names of Samsuditana, followed by traces of a year 30 (or 31) and then blank text (FEIGIN and LANDSBERGER 1955, 159). According to Kinglist B (GRAYSON 1980-83, 100), he ruled 31 years. The latter number (as well as that of Ammiṣaduqa = 21 y.) may be inaccurate, however, because in seven of the nine cases that can be checked against date lists, the lengths of reign given in Kinglist B are incorrect.

324 EDZARD 1957, 18-25 ; STOL 1976, 6-18, 29-31.

325 Following BRINKMAN 1977, 336-337.

326 The reader should note that Huber's calculations (High Chronology) allow only 351 years between Ibbi-Sîn's penultimate year (-2052) and Ammiṣaduqa year 1 (-1701), a span of time that is correspondingly even more difficult to bring into agreement with the most commonly accepted lengths of reign.

327 Other schemes have been proposed by JACOBSEN (1953 [Ibbi-Sîn 24 = Išbi-Irra 13]), SOLLBERGER (1954-56 [Ibbi-Sîn 24 = Išbi-Irra 14]), KIENAST (1965 [Ibbi-Sîn 24 = Išbi-Irra 14]), VAN DIJK (1978 [Ibbi-Sîn 24 = Išbi-Irra 14 or 15]), and VAN DE MIEROOP (1987, 2-3, followed by SIGRIST 1988, 4 [Ibbi-Sîn 24 = Išbi-Irra 18]). These schemes are all

UET 1 292, a fragmentary date list that begins with year names of Ibbi-Sîn and continues — immediately after a gap in the text — with year names of Išbi-Irra, we arrive at the following attributions for years 11 and 12 of the latter king :[328]

Išbi-Irra 11 (= Ibbi-Sîn 24) :

mu [...] gibil-šè ^{d}*I-bi-*^{d}EN.ZU in-sìg [329] "Year [Išbi-Irra the king] defeated Ibbi-Sîn ..."	= *UET* 1 292 ii 16-18
mu-ús-sa ^{d}*Iš-bi-*^{d}*Ìr-ra* lugal-e ugnim lú-SU.A *ù* Elam bi-in-ra "Year after Išbi-Irra the king smote the army of SU.A and Elam"	= Crawford 11a
mu bàd *Iš*$_{8}$*-tár-tá-ra-am-*^{d}*Iš-bi-Ìr-ra* ba-dù "Year the fortress Ištar-tarâm-Išbi-Irra was built"	= Crawford 11b

Išbi-Irra 12 :

mu (^{d}*Iš-bi-Ìr-ra* lugal-e) $^{d/giš}$šu-nir-gal ^{d}En-líl *ù* ^{d}Nin-urta(-ra) mu-ne/na-dím "Year (Išbi-Irra the king) fashioned a great emblem for Enlil and Ninurta"	= *UET* 1 292 ii 19-21 = Crawford 12b
mu-ús-sa bàd *Iš*$_{8}$*-tár-tá-ra-am-*^{d}*Iš-bi-Ìr-ra* ba-dù "Year after the fortress Ištar-tarâm-Išbi-Irra was built"	= Crawford 12a

When we compare the chronological scheme set forth by BRINKMAN (1977, 336-337), which assumes a synchronism Ibbi-Sîn 24 = Išbi-Irra 13, our proposed synchronism (Ibbi-Sîn 24 = Išbi-Irra 11) extends by 2 years the span of time between the fall of Ur and the first year of Ammiṣaduqa (because of the synchronisms Zambiya 2 = Sîn-iqīšam 5, Rim-Sîn I 60 = Hammurabi 30, etc.).

This time-span is lengthened 1 more year if we assume that Warad-Sîn reigned 13 years instead of 12, as indeed seems to be the case.[330]

---

based on the date list of Išbi-Irra from Tell Harmal published by TAHA BAQIR (1948), who supposed that 1, 2, or 3 year names may have been missing in the break at the very top of the list before the first preserved formula, which he identified as that of year x + 1. Of course, two (or more) of the year formulae before his x + 11 (including the 1, 2, or 3 in the break) may refer to a single year.

328 Compare the analysis of JACOBSEN (1953, 43-44). For Crawford's system, see VAN DE MIEROOP 1987, 2-3, where it is recapitulated alongside his own.

329 CRAWFORD (1954), JACOBSEN (1953, 43), SOLLBERGER (1954-56, 38-42), and EDZARD (1957, 24) accept this as a year formula of Išbi-Irra, while VAN DIJK (1978, 202-205), SIGRIST 1988 (4, 13-21), and apparently VAN DE MIEROOP (1987, 2-3) prefer to assign it to Ibbi-Sîn.

330 STOL 1976, 18.

If we follow the reckoning described above, 361 known years separated the 24th and final year of Ibbi-Sîn and the first year of Ammiṣaduqa. If we further assume that the eclipse associated with Ibbi-Sîn's downfall took place in his penultimate year, then 362 known years separated that event, which we have been able to date to 1912 BC, from Ammiṣaduqa's first year. Year 1 of Ammiṣaduqa, then, began in 1550 BC, which, as we have already seen, falls exactly where it should in the 8-year cycle of Venus appearances. Finally, we note that in identifying 1912 BC as Ibbi-Sîn's penultimate year, we equate 1954 BC, the year of the earlier eclipse, with the penultimate year of Šulgi.

5.3. BABYLON'S COLLAPSE AND REVIVAL

Following the scheme outlined above, and assuming that Ammiṣaduqa and Samsuditana reigned 21 years and 31 years respectively,[331] the fall of Babylon occurred in 1499 BC.

Evidence from East of the Tigris (Tell Muḥammad, Baghdad)

Excavations carried out by the Iraqi State Organization for Antiquities and Heritage at Tell Muḥammad,[332] a large mound south of Tell Harmal in southeastern Baghdad, have the potential to add significantly to our knowledge of the era immediately following the fall of Babylon. Seven archaeological levels were said to be identified in the excavations. The highest of these, Level I, has been attributed to the beginning of the Kassite Period,[333] while Levels II-VII have been called "Old Babylonian."[334] Although nothing substantive has been reported about the character or finds of Level I, a temple and a number of houses were uncovered in Levels II-IV.[335]

In the pottery registered as coming from Levels III and II of Tell Muḥammad, Gasche has identified forms similar to the typical Late Old Babylonian shapes attested at Tell ed-Dēr down to about thirty years before the fall of Babylon.[336] Additionally he has identified from unspecified proveniences at Tell Muḥammad both jars (cf. Pl. 2 : 6)[337] and goblets (cf. Pl. 1 : 8) like those of the earliest Kassite assemblages at Tell ed-Dēr. Thus, even though the available stratigraphic information is regrettably incomplete, Tell Muḥammad has produced a series of vessel shapes that, based on comparison with those of northern Babylonia, extends from the Late Old Babylonian Period into the Early Kassite.

---

331 See n. 323 above.

332 Several short reports summarize the progress of the Iraqi excavations : *Iraq* 41 (1979), 156 ; *Iraq* 43 (1981), 184 ; *Iraq* 45 (1983), 216 ; *Iraq* 47 (1985), 223 ; *AfO* 29-30 (1983-84), 218 ; *AfO* 34 (1987), 218 ; and *Sumer* 39 (1983), 15.
SARRE and HERZFELD (1920, vol. 2, 95-96) provide a sketch-map of Tell Muḥammad and a brief description of its topography. ADAMS (1965, 50 and 174, nn. 26-29 ; 152, No. 414) discusses the site and summarizes the results of earlier investigators. See also WALL-ROMANA (1990) for a possible identification with Agade.

333 *AfO* 34 (1987), 218. In *Iraq* 43 (1981), 184, the upper level is referred to simply as Kassite.

334 The main occupation of the site was attributed to the Isin-Larsa Period after the first season's work in 1978 (*Iraq* 41 [1979], 156). By 1981, Levels II-IV were being described as Old Babylonian (*Iraq* 43 [1981], 184). In an M.A. thesis presented in 1985, Levels II-VII were called Old Babylonian (*AfO* 34 [1987], 218).

335 ADIBA ALAMUDDIN AL-KHAYYAT (1984 [Arabic]) has published a group of terracotta figurines from Level II.

336 GASCHE 1989b, 119.

337 Cf. also MINSAER 1991, Pl. 14 : 2-12.

This ceramic sequence provides an archeological context for the epigraphic discoveries from Tell Muḫammad, which, as it turns out, reveal critical new information about Babylon's fate in the aftermath of the First Dynasty's collapse. Economic texts in Old-Babylonian style were recovered from both Levels III and II, some thirty of which have been studied by Iman Jamil al-Ubaid.[338] These texts have year names otherwise unknown in the corpus of Old Babylonian date formulae. A number of texts from Level II bear a year formula that is particularly significant in the present context : MU.x.KÁM(.MA) *ša* KÁ.DINGIR.RA.KI *uš-bu*, most plausibly to be translated "year x that Babylon was resettled."[339] Eleven citations of this formula occur in these texts, with the year-number ranging between 30 and 41 (for the year-numbers 10? and 48?, see respectively n. 350 and n. 348 below). Such a formula, occurring in texts that are otherwise characteristically Old Babylonian,[340] can plausibly refer only to a period of time after the reign of the last Old Babylonian king, Samsuditana. The apparent documentary gap between the end of the Old Babylonian Period and c. 1400 [341] is therefore narrowed by these texts. The following are the various attestations of the formula :

MU.10?.KÁM *ša* KÁ.DINGIR.RA.KI *uš-bu* (beginning of formula damaged)

MU.30(+x).KÁM.MA *ša* KÁ.DINGIR.RA.KI *uš-bu*

MU.36.KÁM.MA *ša* KÁ.DINGIR.RA.KI *uš-bu*

MU.37.KÁM.MA *ša* KÁ.DINGIR.RA.KI *uš-bu*

MU.38.KÁM.MA *ša* KÁ.DINGIR.RA.KI *uš-bu* —> IM 92134 —>

MU.39.KÁM.MA *ša* KÁ.DINGIR.RA.KI *uš-bu*

MU.40(+x).KÁM.MA *ša* KÁ.DINGIR.RA.KI *uš-bu*

MU.41.KÁM.MA *ša* KÁ.DINGIR.RA.KI *uš-bu*

MU.48?.KÁM.MA *ša* KÁ.DINGIR.RA.KI *uš-bu* (beginning of formula damaged)

338 Hand-copies and transliterations of these texts appear in IMAN JAMIL AL-UBAID's University of Baghdad master's thesis (1983 [Arabic]). The authors express their deepest gratitude for being permitted to use her work in this study.

339 Texts bearing this formula were found in Rooms 22 and 119 of Level II, as well as in unspecified Level II contexts, according to Iman Jamil al-Ubaid's catalog (1983, 89-110).

340 These texts share many characteristics with the late Old Babylonian texts from Tell ed-Dēr (we thank M. Tanret and C. Janssen for this observation). For example, they employ certain legal phrases that are typically Old Babylonian : e.g., *ana nāši kanīkišu*, "to the bearer of his sealed document" (IM 92134 : 8 ; 92135 : 11 ; 92138 : 11 ; etc.), which occurs regularly in loan contracts from the reign of Ammiditana onwards (SKAIST 1994, 191-192, 200) ; and *ana* ITI.x.KAM, "within x month(s)" (IM 92134 : 7 ; 92137 : 7 ; 92138 : 10 ; etc.), which occurs in late OB texts from Babylon and Sippar (SKAIST 1994, 168).

341 The latest available Old Babylonian document is dated to Samsuditana year 26 or 27 (KLENGEL 1983, No. 77 ; WALKER 1978, 236-237). The earliest available Kassite texts are dated around 1400, and include building inscriptions of Kara-indaš (BRINKMAN 1976, 169-171, N.2.1-N.2.2), a seal inscription of his son (BRINKMAN 1976, 171, N.2.3), an incomplete Early Kassite inscription of uncertain chronological significance (SASSMANNSHAUSEN 1994), a legal text dated to the reign of Kadašman-Ḫarbe I (BRINKMAN 1976, 146, K^{a}.2.1 ; 388, Text 18), another dated to the reign of either Kadašman-Ḫarbe I or Kadašman-Enlil I (BRINKMAN 1976, 144, J.5.5 ; 391, Text 23), and an economic text from the reign of Kurigalzu I (BRINKMAN 1976, 239-240, Q.2.115.168, and p. 402, published later by DONBAZ 1987, D. 85).

The translation of *ušbu* as "resettled" is based on parallels found in the omen collections.[342] In all the parallels known, the toponym in question is said or implied to have been first abandoned or devastated (or predicted to be) before being resettled :

URU.BI *innaddīma ul uššab*
"That city will be abandoned and will not be resettled" (*CT* 39 10 :24)

ālāni ḫarbūte uššabū
"The devastated cities will be resettled" (*KAR* 2 423 ii 7)

KI.BI *iḫarrumma ana arkât ūmī uššab*
"This locality will fall into ruins, but in the future it will be resettled" (*CT* 39 21 :168)

[*mā*]*tu nadītu uššab*
"The abandoned land will be resettled" (*CT* 31 19 :16)

mātu ša šulputat uššab
"The land that has been devastated will be resettled" (*TCL* 6 10 :19)

nārum lā ḫerītum iḫḫerri kišāssa šubtam uššab
"The undredged canal will be dredged ; its bank will be resettled with habitation" (*YOS* 10 17 :40)

šubāt namê nadûti ina amāt ^{d}*Enlil uššabū*
"By the command of Enlil, the settlements in the abandoned countryside will be reinhabited" (*ABL* 1080 : 7- rev. 1 = *SAA* 10 No. 55 : 7'- rev. 1)

In the year formula in question, therefore, the occurrence of (*w*)*ašābu*(*m*) with Babylon as the subject implies that Babylon was first abandoned and then resettled. This abandonment and resettlement most plausibly refers, respectively, to a depopulation of the capital consequent to the Hittite attack under Muršili I and a later repopulation under the Kassites.

As can be seen from the table below, which lists all the various year formulae found in the Tell Muḫammad texts studied by Iman Jamil al-Ubaid,[343] the Babylon dates appear as part of a dual dating procedure, in which two equivalent year names were written on different edges of a tablet.[344] The older texts of Level III (and several documents from the later Level II) were dated by what appears to have been an indigenous system. Then there was a change : Level II documents began to be dated both by the indigenous year formulae and the Babylon formulae. Finally, the indigenous system was abandoned. The following are the attestations presently known :

342 In Akkadian, when a toponym functions as the subject of (*w*)*ašābu*(*m*) — as in the formula in question — the verb must be translated "to be (re)settled, (re)populated" (see *CAD* A/2, pp. 403-404 sub *ašābu* 3b ; *AHw*, pp. 1482-83 mng. 6).

343 IM 90605, 90606_2, 90608, 90610, 90611, 90617, 92723, 92730, 92734, also treated by Iman Jamil al-Ubaid, bear no year formulae. In addition, IM 90593 mentions only "day 24" and possibly a month name, which is broken.

344 When the bottom edge was used, the tablet was reversed, so that the date would not be confused with the continuation of the text of the document.

IM	*Year formula*	*text type*	*level*
90602	Year in which water carried King Ḫurduzum, ..., up to the city.	loan of silver	III
90603	Year in which Ṣilli-Adad, son of Šumma-ilu, was killed.	disbursement of grain	III
90606_1	Year in which Ḫurduzum refurbished the gods of Ešnunna.	purchase of empty lot	III
90615	Year in which he brought the *mayyāru*-plows.	loan of silver	III
90616	Year in which Naḫlim returned from Assur.	loan of grain	III
90590	Year in which Zalmi^{ki} was conquered.[345]	—	—
92137	Year of the devastating flood in Dūr-Banâya and (when) sesame was in demand (/planted).	loan of silver	II
92138	Year in which Ninnaḫneru, son of Burna-Saḫ, died.	loan of silver	II
92732	Year in which the son of Udaša-x died.	loan of grain	II
92725	Year the son of Ḫurbaḫ initiated hostilities with the king.[346]	disbursement of grain	II
92721	(1) Year 36 that Babylon was resettled. (2) Year in which the son of Ḫurbaḫ was killed in Tupliaš.	loan of grain	II
92728	(1) Year 37 that Babylon was resettled. (2) Year in which King Šiptaulzi ...	loan of grain	II
92134	(1) Year 38 that Babylon was resettled. (2) Year in which "fruit" (i.e. the moon) was eclipsed.[347] Month of Abu (July-August), Day 10	loan of silver	II
92139	(1) Year 38 that Babylon was resettled.[348] (2) Year in which the moon became invisible, an eclipse occurred.[349] Month of Nisannu (March-April), [Day x]	loan of silver	II
92722	(1) Year 38 that Babylon was resettled. (2) Year in which Bēl-aḫḫīšu and AN-šumun died.	loan of silver, grain	II
92135	(1) Year 39 that Babylon was resettled. (2) Year in which PN, son of PN_2, ...	loan of silver, grain, chick peas	II
92720	(1) Year 30(+x) that Babylon was resettled. (2) Year in which King Šiptaulzi ...	disbursement of grain	II
92719	(1) Year [x] that Babylon was resettled.[350] (2) [Year in which] Burna-Saḫ, son of PN_2, ...	disbursement of grain	II

345 Only the date formula of IM 90590 is treated in Iman Jamil al-Ubaid's thesis.

346 Iman Jamil al-Ubaid's reading GÁL.DI.AŠ (meaning unknown) has been interpreted rather as *ig-de-rù*.

347 The reading GIŠ.x is probably to be emended to ⌜GURUN⌝ (*inbu*), not only because it fits the traces, but also because the N-stem of *adāru* (in the meaning "to become eclipsed") demands as its grammatical subject a word referring to a celestial body (compare *CAD* A/1, p. 107 s.v. mng. 8). Compare also ^{d}*Inbi innadirma*, "the 'fruit' was eclipsed" (*YOS* 1 45 i 9).

348 Iman Jamil al-Ubaid reads "48" ; but collation (L. De Meyer and M. Tanret) shows that she mistakenly interpreted one of the last *Winkelhakens* of the broken [M]U-sign ("year") to be part of the following number — hence we have subtracted the numerical value of one *Winkelhaken* (= 10) from 48.

349 Iman Jamil al-Ubaid reads *i-du-ru*, but collation of the text (L. De Meyer and M. Tanret) shows that her copy (*i-aḫ-ru*) is correct (this form stands for *i''aḫru*, the N-stem preterite, subjunctive, of *aḫāru*, which in the G-stem means "to be delayed"). The N-stem of this verb is unattested elsewhere, but it should probably have an ingressive sense, "to become invisible," especially when we compare it with the meaning of the D-stem *uḫḫuru*, "to remain invisible," which is the stem of the verb otherwise found in the lunar eclipse omina and other astronomical report texts (see, for example, ROCHBERG-HALTON 1988, *passim* ; see also *AHw*, p. 18 s.v. ; and cf. *CAD* A/1, p. 170 s.v.).

350 Iman Jamil al-Ubaid reads "10," but the context is broken.

92731	Year 41 that Babylon was resettled.	loan of grain	II
92729	Year 40(+x) that Babylon was resettled.	loan(?) of grain	II
92733	Year [x] that Babylon was resettled.	disbursement of grain	II

The transition from an indigenous system of dating to one marking the years since the resettlement of Babylon indicates that the inhabitants of the lower Diyala region (where Tell Muḫammad is located) had redirected their political allegiance toward the old capital to the south. The object of their allegiance was in all likelihood the Kassite king of Babylon.[351]

If Babyon fell in 1499 BC, as we believe, then the lunar eclipse recorded in the two Tell Muḫammad date formulae listed above could not have occurred before 1462 BC (-1461). From the period shortly before and after this date Gurzadyan has identified the following eclipses that could have been seen in Babylonia :

Total eclipses	*Partial eclipses*	*Occultations*	*No eclipses between* :
	-1442 Jan. 21 and Dec.13	0.01 and 0.02	
-1443 Jul. 28		1.2 [352]	
-1444 Aug. 8		1.1	
-1444 Feb. 13		1.05	
			-1446 Sep. 28 and -1444 Feb. 13
	-1446 Sep. 28	0.25	
-1447 Apr. 15		**1.65**	
			-1450 June 16 and -1447 Apr. 15
	-1450 June 16	0.9	
-1451 Dec. 22		1.25	
-1451 June 27		**1.35**	
			-1454 Aug. 28 and -1451 June 27
-1454 Aug. 28		1.45	
-1455 March 16		1.15	
			-1458 May 16 and -1455 March 16
-1458 May 16 (1459 BC)		**1.75**	
			-1461 Jul. 18 and -1458 May 16
-1461 Jul. 18		1.1	
-1461 Jan. 22		1.2	
-1462 Jul. 29		1.2	
-1462 Feb. 1		1.1	
			-1465 Sept. 28 and -1462 Feb. 1
-1465 Sept. 28		1.45	
-1465 Apr. 5		1.52	
	2 partial eclipses in -1466		
			-1469 Dec. 11 and -1466
-1469 Dec. 11		1.25	
-1470 Dec. 22		1.3	

351 However, a Sealand king can not be ruled out.

352 An occultation of over 1.0 is a total eclipse.

Our attention is drawn in particular to the three eclipses shown in bold in the table above. Each had a high degree of occultation and each was preceded by a period of nearly three years during which no eclipses occurred at all, a combination of circumstances that might have led to the commemoration of an eclipse in a year name. We suggest that the earliest eclipse of the three, that of -1458 (1459 BC), which had the highest degree of occultation, was the one that occasioned the year formulae in question.[353] The two other eclipses cannot be excluded from consideration on this account, but the later the eclipse, the later it would have been that Babylon was resettled. And the later we place that event, the less time remains in the fifteenth century for the consolidation of Kassite power throughout lower Mesopotamia. Thus, if the eclipse that was commemorated in the year formulae for 1458 BC occurred in 1459 BC, then Babylon was resettled in 1496 BC (1458 + 38), in other words, 3 years after the date we propose for its fall.

The Early Years of Kassite Rule

Less than a century separated the fall of Babylon in 1499 BC, and the accession of Kara-indaš, in whose reign amicable relations were initiated between the Babylonian and Egyptian courts,[354] thus confirming Babylonia as one of the great powers of southwest Asia. In the intervening period, therefore, the Kassites seized control of Babylon and expanded their dominion over the entire region between the Lower Zab and the Gulf (calling their new realm Karduniaš). The fall of Babylon must have been the occasion of their expansion. What slim evidence there is for these formative years during which the Kassites consolidated their power is found in the Synchronistic History, the Chronicle of Early Kings, and perhaps also the seventh-century inscription attributed to Agum-kakrime — evidence to which we now turn.

In the first quarter of the fifteenth century, Burna-Buriaš I seems to have expanded Kassite control toward the territory under the control of Puzur-Aššur III, king of Assyria, since the two kings are said to have fixed the boundary between them.[355] Afterward, both a brother and son of a succeeding Kassite monarch, Kaštiliaš(u), campaigned in the opposite direction, in the Sealand.[356] The brother — Ulam-Buraš — is probably to be identified with the Ula-Burariaš who is called elsewhere the "son of Burna-Burariaš."[357] The son — Agum — is perhaps to be identified with the famous Agum-kakrime.

We posit that the seventh-century scribe(s) who copied the inscription of this Agum (the only inscription of this king that is known) incorrectly attributed to him the genealogy of an earlier Agum (perhaps because that portion of the original was broken).[358] We also suggest that other evidence in

---

353 We presume that the eclipse mentioned in the Tell Muḥammad texts was total.

354 As stated in a letter of Burna-Buriaš II to Akhenaton (KNUDTZON 1915, No. 10 : 8-10 ; translated by MORAN 1992, No. 10).

355 GRAYSON 1975, 158-159, col. i 5'-7' (Synchronistic History) ; BRINKMAN 1976, 101, n. 8.

356 GRAYSON 1975, 156 : 12-18 (Chronicle of Early Kings).

357 This is according to inscriptions found both at Babylon and Metsamor (Armenia). The first identifies Ula-Burariaš as "king of the Sealand" (WEISSBACH 1903, 7 and Pl. 1, No. 3). The second identifies Burna-Burariaš, father of Ula-Burariaš, as "king" (KHANZADYAN 1983 ; SARKISYAN and DIAKONOFF 1983).

358 This is likely to have been true of the section of Chronicle P dealing with Kurigalzu II, where the writer erred by inserting the genealogy of the earlier Kurigalzu for that of the later king of this name (BRINKMAN 1976, 420-421).

the Agum-kakrime inscription indicates that this king ruled during the period when the Kassites occupied Babylon and were consolidating their power over the South.

Agum-kakrime is said to have returned the statue of Marduk to Babylon from the region of Ḫani, where the Hittites presumably left it after their raid.[359] According to the Marduk Prophecy text, the period of the god's exile was 24 years.[360] Remembering that the Babylon year formulae in the documents from Tell Muḫammad cluster between 36 and 41 years after "Babylon was resettled," we see a new significance in the epithets claimed by Agum-kakrime :

> (I am) king of the Kassites and the Akkadians, king of the broad land of Babylon, the one who (re)settled the land of Ešnunna with an extensive population, king of Padan and Alman, king of the Gutians ...[361]

The chronology of events we have proposed here has the new Kassite rulers consolidating their rule over Babylonia in the immediate aftermath of the collapse of the First Dynasty, with Burna-Buriaš I fixing his northern border with Puzur-Aššur III of Assyria very shortly after its demise. The Kassite king's action implies a significant degree of political control and social stability at least in northern Babylonia and its northern periphery. Such relatively stable social conditions a mere twenty-five years after Babylon's fall are consistent with what we have deduced from the survival and continuing evolution of the Babylonian pottery-making tradition, namely that the breakdown of the social order at the end of the Old Babylonian Period was far from complete, and that the period of instability and dislocation was of relatively short duration. We should perhaps understand the fall of Babylon not as marking the onset of a period of disorder, but instead as signaling the end of a long, slow breakdown and the beginning of an era of political resurgence under energetic new rulers.

5.4. THE NEW CHRONOLOGICAL MARKERS

The analysis that has led to the identification of the new chronological markers for the early second millennium takes into account a vast array of archaeological and textual evidence. Thousands of discrete data were examined and then fitted into a coherent scheme that not only would account for every item, but also could resolve enigmas and seeming contradictions and provide a solid, reliable framework in which to place evidence that has yet to be adduced. The analogy of a picture puzzle is apt.

To be sure, sections of this puzzle had been put together before, thanks to the efforts of those who previously undertook the task. But their work was most often done in isolation, using one type of puzzle-piece only (usually textual but sometimes also astronomical). In contrast, we examined the puzzle from several different vantage points and developed solutions in cooperation, as members of a team with individual areas of expertise. We then analyzed the various categories of archaeological, textual, and astronomical data as a whole. The resulting new symbiosis could not have been achieved if these categories had been treated separately.

---

359 The account of Agum's return of the statue is found in PINCHES 1880, No. 33, col. i 44-col. ii 17.

360 BORGER 1971, 5, col. i 13-17.

361 PINCHES 1880, No. 33, col. i 31-38.

In the two tables that follow we summarize the results of our investigation and show how they affect the chronological relationships among the principal dynasties of southern Mesopotamia in the second millennium.

Suggested date for the formula "year 38 that Babylon was resettled" :[1]	1458 BC	
	38 years	
Suggested date for the resettlement of Babylon :	1496 BC	
Most probable date for the Fall of Babylon :	1499 BC	
	51 years[2]	
Ammiṣaduqa year 1 :	**1550 BC**	
	361 years[3]	
Fall of Ur :	1911 BC	
Eclipse predicting the fall of Ur :[4]		**1912 BC**
		41 years, 9 months
Death of Šulgi :	1953 BC	
Eclipse predicting the death of Šulgi :[5]		**1954 BC**

1) This date-formula is found on two tablets from Tell Muḫammad that also bear year names referring to an eclipse that can be reasonably identified with the eclipse of 16 May 1459 BC.

2) Assuming a 21-year reign for Amiṣaduqa and a 31-year reign for Samsuditana.

3) BRINKMAN (1977, 336-7) gives 359 or 358 years (see p. 346, n. 3) between the fall of Ur and Ammiṣaduqa, year 1. The difference of 3 years is due to his assumption of a synchronism Ibbi-Sîn 24 = Išbi-Irra 13 (compared with our proposal of Ibbi-Sîn 24 = Išbi-Irra 11), and due to his attribution of 12 years to Warad-Sîn (compared with our 13).

4) We assume that this eclipse occurred in Ibbi-Sîn's penultimate year.

5) If we assume that the Ibbi-Sîn eclipse occurred in his penultimate year, then this eclipse must have taken place in Šulgi's penultimate year as well.

Legend for Table on p. 91 :

Linked by synchronisms to the Assyrian sequence, which is reconstructed on the basis of the AKL, eponym lists, and eponym chronicle and anchored by the *solar eclipse of June 763 BC* (= eponymy of Bur-Saggilê ; see MILLARD 1994, 41 and UNGNAD 1938b, 414). Regnal dates are 5 years lower than BRINKMAN (1977, 338) because of our acceptance of the hypothesis that the Assyrians used a lunar calendar without intercalary months before Tiglath-pileser I (see BRINKMAN 1976, 32, n. 89).

Dated by reference to the *Ur III eclipses and the 8-year cycle of Venus* (Middle Chronology –96 years) and on the basis of the following assumptions : 1) the total duration of Babylon I = 300 years, Larsa = 264 years, Isin I = 224 years ; 2) Išbi-Irra 11 = Ibbi-Sîn 24 (see pp. 81-82 above) ; Lipit-Ištar 11 = Gungunum 10 ; Ur-Ninurta 1 = Gungunum 11 ; Būr-Sîn 1 = Sumuel 1 ; Zambīya 2 = Sîn-iqīšam 5 (STOL 1976, 14-15, 26, 29-30) ; Rīm-Sîn I 60 = Hammurabi 30 (EDZARD 1957, 22-24) ; 3) the time-span between the ocurrence of the eclipse predicting the fall of Ur (–1911 = 1912 BC = penultimate year of Ibbi-Sîn [see below]) and Ammiṣaduqa year 1 (–1551 = 1550 BC, fixed to the 8-year Venus cycle) is 362 years (see above, p. 83).

Anchored by the *Ur III lunar eclipses* (Middle Chronology –94 years) with regnal dates based on the following assumptions : 1) Ibbi-Sîn reigned 24 years (Ur-Isin Kinglist, *SKL* mss. WB and J vs. the 25 years of *SKL* mss. P_3 and Su_1), and the eclipse predicting the fall of Ur occurred in his penultimate year (–1911 = 1912 BC) ; 2) Šu-Sîn and Amar-Sîn reigned 9 years each ; 3) Šulgi reigned 48 years, and the eclipse predicting his death occurred in his penultimate year (–1953 = 1954 BC) ; 4) Ur-Nammu reigned 18 years.

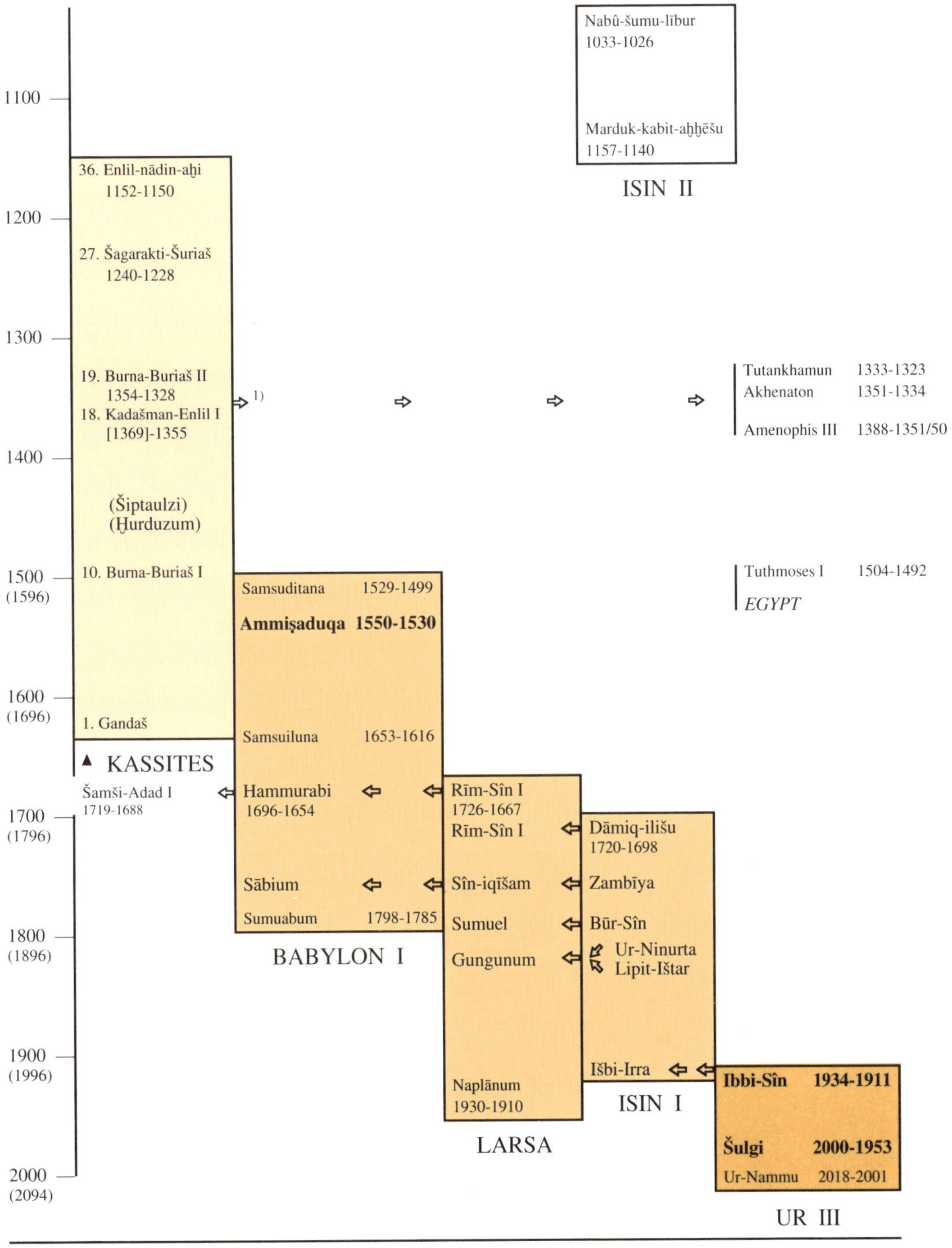

Principal Southern Mesopotamian Dynasties of the Second Millennium and Their Dating

(1596) (2094) Middle Chronology dates.

⇦ Synchronism (or indirect synchr. [Sîn-iqīšam/Sābium]).

1) For the synchronisms with Egypt, see p. 66, n. 272. Tuthmoses I is introduced here because of his activities against the Mitannians.

While we do not claim to have solved all the problems of second-millennium chronology, we believe that the scheme set forth here is the most credible one that can be elaborated at present. All the pieces are in place and they interlock. Questions about where to fix synchronisms between Ibbi-Sîn and Išbi-Irra, how to choose between the variants for the reign-lengths of Ibbi-Sîn and Warad-Sîn, and other questions have been answered by the absolute necessity of respecting two unchangeable eclipse anchors — one fixed in 1954 BC, and the other 41 years and 9 months later, in 1912 — and by the unalterable fact that the first year of Ammiṣaduqa must be tied to the 8-year cycle of Venus. One has to choose 1550 for the first year of this king not only because it best accords with presently attested synchronisms and reign-length figures but also because it fits the 8-year cycle.[362]

The internal arrangement of these data may change, but not the frame that gives them structure. Even if evidence is eventually uncovered proving beyond doubt that Ibbi-Sîn year 24 is to be matched with, for example, Išbi-Irra 14 instead of year 11, or that Warad-Sîn definitely reigned 12 years instead of 13, or if any other synchronism or reign-length from this time-span proves in need of adjustment, that adjustment will have to be made within the immutable framework provided by the eclipse anchors and the 8-year cycle of Venus appearances.

5.5. Chronological Implications for Other Periods and Regions

Finally, we cannot fail to highlight at this point, at least briefly, the repercussions that our proposed new dates have for earlier dynasties, since they require not only a lowering of all Babylonian dynasties ranging back to the beginning of Ur III (= 2018 BC), but also of reigns before this time. Thus, if we follow the scheme proposed by HALLO (1957-71), the Dynasty of Akkad would have terminated around the beginning of Ur III, and its commencement would have to be set at about 2200 BC.[363]

Moreover, every piece of evidence with historical significance from the Near East belonging to the earlier part of the second millennium and dated by reference to Babylonian chronology will have to be adapted. This includes, but is by no means limited to, evidence for the relevant Elamite dynasties, the Old Hittite Kingdom, and the Levant in the Middle Bronze Age. The repercussions are therefore far-reaching. An analysis of them, however, is beyond the scope of the present investigation, as is any analysis of the chronological relationship between the activities of Tuthmoses I and Muršili I in Syria and the number and lengths of the generations that separated Muršili I and Tudḫaliya I.

---

362 The choice of 1558 (= year 1 of Ammiṣaduqa in the so-called "Ultra-low" Chronology) would shorten the span between Ibbi-Sîn and Ammiṣaduqa too much, making it even more difficult to reconcile all the attested year formulae with the regnal periods attested in the kinglist, while the choice of 1542 would lengthen it to the point of irreconcilability.

363 We judge Hallo's scheme to be more reasonable than the traditional one, which fixes the end of this dynasty at 2154 BC (the date cited, e.g., in BRINKMAN 1977, 336; cf. also p. 346, n. 1). See also VALLAT 1997a. The attempt of GLASSNER (1994) to reduce the span of time between the end of the reign of Šar-kali-šarrī and the beginning of the reign of Ur-Nammu from c. 40 years to c. 30 years is an interesting suggestion but, unfortunately, has no firm basis in the available evidence.

ABBREVIATIONS AND BIBLIOGRAPHY *

ABL = HARPER, R.F., 1892-1914

ADAMS, R.McC., 1965 : *Land Behind Baghdad. A History of Settlement on the Diyala Plains*, Chicago, London.

ADAMS, R.McC., 1981 : *Heartland of Cities. Surveys of Ancient Settlement and Land Use on the Central Floodplain of the Euphrates*, Chicago.

ADIBA ALAMUDDIN AL-KHAYYAT, 1984 : « Study of a Number of Terracottas of Tell Muhammad », *Sumer* 43, 146-154 (Arabic).

AL-GAILANI-WERR, L., 1965 : « Tell edh-Dhiba'i », *Sumer* 21, 33-40.

AMIET, P., 1988 : *Suse. 6000 ans d'histoire*, Paris.

ARMSTRONG, J.A., 1989 : *The Archaeology of Nippur from the Decline of the Kassite Kingdom Until the Rise of the Neo-Babylonian Empire*, PhD, University of Chicago.

ARMSTRONG, J.A., 1992 : « West of Edin : Tell al-Deylam and the Babylonian City of Dilbat », *BiblAr* 55, 219-226.

ARMSTRONG, J.A., 1993 : « Pottery » *in* ZETTLER, R.L., *Nippur* III : *Kassite Buildings in Area WC-1* (= *OIP* 111), Chicago, 67-80.

ARMSTRONG, J.A., BRANDT, M.C., 1994 : « Ancient Dunes at Nippur » *in* GASCHE, H. *et al.* (Ed.), *Cinquante-deux réflexions sur le Proche-Orient ancien offertes en hommage à Léon De Meyer* (= *MHEO* 2), Leuven, 255-263.

ARO, J., 1970 : « Mittelbabylonische Kleidertexte der Hilprecht-Sammlung, Jena. Mit einem Anhang : Fünf alt-, mittel- und neubabylonische Texte verschiedenen Inhalts aus der gleichen Sammlung (= *BSGW* 115/2), Berlin.

AR-RAWI, F.N.H., 1993 : « A New Old Babylonian Date List from Sippir with Year Names of Apil-Sîn and Sîn-muballiṭ », *ZA* 83, 22-30.

ÅSTRÖM, P. (Ed.), 1987 : *High, Middle or Low ? Acts of an International Colloquium on Absolute Chronolgy Held at the University of Gothenburg 20th-22nd August 1987*. Part 1, Gothenburg.

BAQIR : see TAHA BAQIR

BE VI/1 = RANKE, H., 1906

BERGAMINI, G., 1984 : « The Excavations in Tell Yelkhi », *Sumer* 40, 224-244.

BERGAMINI *et al.* 1985 = BERGAMINI, G., SAPORETTI, C., COSTANTINI, L., COSTANTINI BIASINI, L., MASIERO, C., 1985 : « Tell Yelkhi », *La terra tra i due fiumi. Venti anni di archeologia italiana in Medio Oriente. La Mesopotamia dei tesori*, Torino, 41-60.

* The abbreviations used here and in the preceding chapters are those recommended in *Northern Akkad Project Reports* 8 (Ghent, 1993), 49-65.

BIROT, M., 1978 : Review of DALLEY, S., WALKER, C.B.F., HAWKINS, J.D., 1976 : *The Old Babylonian Tablets from Tell al-Rimah*, London, *in RA* 72, 181-190.

BIROT, M., 1985 : « Les chroniques "Assyriennes" de Mari », *MARI* 4, 219-242.

BOEHMER, R.M., DÄMMER, H.-W., 1985 : *Tell Imlihiye, Tell Zubeidi, Tell Abbas* (= *BaF* 7), Mainz.

BOESE, J., WILHELM, G., 1979 : « Aššur-dān I, Ninurta-apil-Ekur und die mittelassyrische Chronologie », *WZKM* 71, 19-38.

BORGER, R., 1956 : *Die Inschriften Asarhaddons Königs von Assyrien* (= *AfO Beih.* 9), Graz.

BORGER, R., 1971 : « Gott Marduk und Gott-König Šulgi als Propheten. Zwei prophetische Texte », *BiOr* 28, 3-24.

BRINKMAN, J.A., 1968 : *A Political History of Post-Kassite Babylonia 1158-722 B.C.* (= *AnOr* 43), Roma.

BRINKMAN, J.A., 1972 : « Foreign Relations of Babylonia from 1600 to 625 B.C. : the Documentary Evidence », *AJA* 76, 271-281.

BRINKMAN, J.A., 1973 : « Comments on the Nassouhi Kinglist and the Assyrian Kinglist Tradition », *Or* 42, 306-319.

BRINKMAN, J.A., 1976 : *Materials and Studies for Kassite History* 1. *A Catalogue of Cuneiform Sources Pertaining to Specific Monarchs of the Kassite Dynasty*, Chicago.

BRINKMAN, J.A., 1977 : « Mesopotamian Chronology of the Historical Period », Appendix to OPPENHEIM, A.L., *Ancient Mesopotamia. Portrait of a Dead Civilization* (rev. ed. completed by E. Reiner), Chicago, 335-348.

BRINKMAN, J.A., 1984 : « Settlement Surveys and Documentary Evidence : Regional Variation and Secular Trend in Mesopotamian Demography », *JNES* 43, 169-180.

BRINKMAN, J.A., 1993 : « Meerland », *RlA* 8/1-2, 6-10.

BURINGH, P., 1960 : *Soils and Soil Conditions in Iraq*, Baghdad.

CAMERON, G.G., 1936 : *History of Early Iran*, Chicago.

CAMPBELL, E.F., 1979 [1961] : « The Ancient Near East : Chronological Bibliography and Charts » *in* WRIGHT, G.E. (Ed.), *The Bible and the Ancient Near East. Essays in Honor of William Foxwell Albright*, Winona Lake, 214-224.

CARTER, E., 1970 : « Second Millennium Sites in Khūzistān », *Iran* 8, 200-202.

CAVAIGNAC, E., 1955 : « Duppišu », *RA* 49, 204-206.

CAVIGNEAUX, A., ISMAIL, B.K., 1990 : « Die Statthalter von Suḫu und Mari im 8. Jh. v. Chr. anhand neuer Texte aus den irakischen Grabungen im Staugebiet des Qadissiya-Damms », *BaM* 21, 321-456.

CHARPIN, D., 1986 : « Les Elamites à Šubat-Enlil » *in* DE MEYER, L. *et al.* (Ed.), *Fragmenta Historiae Elamicae. Mélanges offerts à M.-J. Steve*, Paris, 129-137.

CHARPIN, D., 1987 : « Šubat-Enlil et le pays d'Apum », *MARI* 5, 129-140.

CHARPIN, D., DURAND, J.-M., 1985 : « La prise du pouvoir par Zimri-Lim », *MARI* 4, 293-342.

CHARPIN, D., DURAND, J.-M., 1991 : « La suzeraineté de l'empereur (Sukkalmaḫ) d'Elam sur la Mésopotamie et le 'nationalisme' amorrite », *Mésopotamie et Elam. Actes de la XXXVIème Rencontre Assyriologique Internationale, Gand, 10-14 juillet 1989* (= *MHEO* 1), Ghent, 59-66.

CHARPIN *et al.* 1988 = CHARPIN, D., JOANNÈS, F., LACKENBACHER, S., LAFONT, B., 1988 : *Archives épistolaires de Mari* I/2 (= *ARM* 26), Paris.

CIVIL, M., 1975 : « Appendix A : Cuneiform Texts » *in* GIBSON, McG., *Excavations at Nippur. Eleventh Season* (= *OIC* 22), Chicago, London, 125-142.

CIVIL, M., 1978 : « Catalogue of Texts », *OIC* 23, 112-125.

CLAY, A.T., 1915 : *Miscellaneous Inscriptions in the Yale Babylonian Collection* (= *YOS* 1), New Haven, London.

COLLON, D., 1988 : *First Impressions. Cylinder Seals in the Ancient Near East*, London.

CORNELIUS, F., 1954-56 : « Die Chronologie des Vorderen Orients im 2. Jahrtausend v. Chr. », *AfO* 17, 294-309.

CRAWFORD, V.E., 1954 : *Sumerian Economic Texts from the First Dynasty of Isin* (= *BIN* 9), New Haven.

CT 31 = HANDCOCK, P.S.P, 1911

CT 39 = GADD, C.J., 1926

DE GENOUILLAC, H., 1910-11 : *Inventaire des tablettes de Tello conservées au Musée Impérial Ottoman*, 2. *Textes d'époque d'Agadé et de l'époque d'Ur*, Paris.

DE GENOUILLAC, H., 1925 : *Fouilles françaises d'el-'Akymer. Premières recherches archéologiques à Kich* 2, Paris.

DE LIAGRE BÖHL, F.M.Th., 1946 : *King Ḫammurabi of Babylon in the Setting of his Time (about 1700 B.C.)* (= *MAW* 9/10), Amsterdam.

DE MEYER, L., 1978 : « Documents épigraphiques paléo-babyloniens provenant des sondages A, B et D », *TD* 2, 147-184.

DE MEYER, L., 1982 : « Les structures politiques en Susiane à l'époque des Sukkalmaḫ », *Les pouvoirs locaux en Mésopotamie et dans les régions adjacentes*, Bruxelles, 92-97.

DELOUGAZ, P., 1952 : *Pottery from the Diyala Region* (= *OIP* 63), Chicago.

DESCHESNE, O., 1996 : « Le bitume dans l'antiquité » *in* CONNAN, J., DESCHESNE, O., *Le bitume à Suse. Collection du Musée du Louvre*, Paris, 18-46.

DONBAZ, V., 1987 : « Two Documents from the Diverse Collections in Istanbul » *in* OWEN, D.I., MORRISON, M.A. (Ed.), *Studies on the Civilization and Culture of Nuzi and the Hurrians* 2 (= *General Studies and Excavations at Nuzi* 9/1), Winona Lake, 69-75.

DURAND, J.-M., 1977 : « Notes sur l'histoire de Larsa (I) », *RA* 71, 17-34.

DURAND, J.-M., 1986 : « Fragments rejoints pour une histoire élamite », *in* DE MEYER, L. *et al.* (Ed.), *Fragmenta Historiae Elamicae. Mélanges offerts à M.-J. Steve*, Paris, 111-128.

DURAND, J.-M., 1995 : « L'empereur d'Elam et ses vassaux », *in* GASCHE, H. *et al.* (Ed.), *Cinquante-deux réflexions sur le Proche-Orient ancien offertes en hommage à Léon De Meyer* (= *MHE OP* 2), Leuven, 15-22.

EBELING, E., 1923 : *Keilschrifttexte aus Assur religiösen Inhalts* 2 (= *WVDOG* 34), Leipzig.

EBELING, E., 1927 : *Keilschrifttexte aus Assur juristischen Inhalts* (= *WVDOG* 50), Leipzig.

EDZARD, D.O., 1957 : *Die »zweite Zwischenzeit« Babyloniens*, Wiesbaden.

FEIGIN, S.I., LANDSBERGER, B., 1955 : « The Date List of the Babylonian King Samsu-ditana », *JNES* 14, 137-160.

FRAME, G., 1995 : *Rulers of Babylonia from the Second Dynasty of Isin to the End of Assyrian Domination (1157-612 BC)* (= *Royal Inscriptions of Mesopotamia. Babylonian Periods* 2), Toronto.

FRANKE, J.A., 1978 : « Area WB », *OIC* 23, 53-106.

FRANKEN, H.J., KALSBEEK, J., 1984 : « Some Techniques Used by the Potters of Tell ed-Dēr », *TD* 4, 81-89.

FRANKFORT, H., 1955 : *Stratified Cylinder Seals from the Diyala Region* (= *OIP* 72), Chicago.

FREYDANK, H., 1991 : *Beiträge zur mittelassyrischen Chronologie und Geschichte* (= *SGKAO* 21), Berlin.

GADD, C.J., 1926 : *Cuneiform Texts from Babylonian Tablets (, &c.,) in the British Museum* 39, London.

GADD, C.J., 1978 : « Hammurabi and the End of his Dynasty », *CAH* 2/1 (2nd ed.), Cambridge, 176-227.

GADD *et al.* 1928 = GADD, C.J., LEGRAIN, E., SMITH, S., 1928 : *Royal Inscriptions* (= *UET* 1), London.

GASCHE, H., 1973 : *La poterie élamite du deuxième millénaire a.C.* (= *MDP* 47), Leiden, Paris.

GASCHE, H., 1978 : « Le Sondage A : l'Ensemble I », *TD* 2, 57-131.

GASCHE, H., 1989a : « Tell ed-Dēr 1988. Un quartier du 17e siècle avant notre ère (Rapport préliminaire). 1. Les fouilles du chantier F », *NAPR* 3, 15-18.

GASCHE, H., 1989b : *La Babylonie au 17e siècle avant notre ère : approche archéologique, problèmes et perspectives* (= *MHEM* 1), Ghent.

GASCHE, H., 1991 : « Tell ed-Dēr 1985-1987. Les vestiges Méso-Babyloniens. I. Les Chantier E, E3 & le Sondage E2 », *NAPR* 6, 11-40.

GELB, I.J., 1954 : « Two Assyrian King Lists », *JNES* 13, 209-230.

GENOUILLAC : see DE GENOUILLAC

GIBSON, McG., 1975 : *Excavations at Nippur. Eleventh Season* (= *OIC* 22), Chicago, London.

GIBSON, McG., 1978a : « Area WA », *OIC* 23, 4-52.

GIBSON, McG., 1978b : « Nippur 1975, A Summary Report », *Sumer* 34, 114-121.

GIBSON, McG., 1980 : « Current Research at Nippur : Ecological, Anthropological and Documentary Interplay », *L'archéologie de l'Iraq du début de l'époque néolithique à 333 avant notre ère*, Paris, 193-205.

GIBSON, McG., 1984 : « 16th Season at Nippur, 1985 », *Sumer* 43, 252-254.

GLASSNER, J.-J., 1993 : *Chroniques mésopotamiennes*, Paris.

GLASSNER, J.-J., 1994 : « La fin d'Akkadē : approche chronologique », *NABU* 9).

GLASSNER, J.-J., 1996 : « Kuk-Kirwaš, sukkalmaḫ », *NABU* 35).

GOETZE, A., 1947 : *Old Babylonian Omen Texts* (= *YOS* 10), New Haven, London.

GRAYSON, A.K., 1975 : *Assyrian and Babylonian Chronicles* (= *TCS* 5), Locust Valley NY, Glückstadt.

GRAYSON, A.K., 1980-83 : « Königslisten und Chroniken. B. Akkadisch », *RlA* 6, 86-135.

GRAYSON, A.K., 1985 : « Rivalry over Rulership at Aššur. The Puzur-Sîn Inscription », *ARRIM* 3, 9-14.

GRAYSON, A.K., 1987 : *Assyrian Rulers of the Third and Second Millennia BC (to 1115 BC)* (= *RIMA* 1), Toronto.

GRAYSON, A.K., 1991 : *Assyrian Rulers of the Early First Millennium BC I (1114-859 BC)* (= *RIMA* 2), Toronto.

GRIMAL, N., 1992 : *A History of Ancient Egypt*, Oxford.

HALLO, W.W., 1957-71 : « Gutium », *RlA* 3, 708-720.

HANDCOCK, P.S.P, 1911 : *Cuneiform Texts from Babylonian Tablets (, &c.,) in the British Museum* 31, London.

Haradum 1 = KEPINSKI-LECOMTE, C. (Ed.), 1992

HARPER, R.F., 1892-1914 : *Assyrian and Babylonian Letters Belonging to the K(ouyunjik) Collection(s) of the British Museum* (14 vols.), Chicago.

HØJLUND, F., 1987 : *The Bronze Age Pottery* (= *Failaka/Dilmun. The Second Millennium Settlements* 2 = *JASP* 17/2), Aarhus, Kuwait.

HØJLUND, F., 1989 : « Dilmun and the Sealand », *NAPR* 2, 9-14.

HØJLUND, F., ANDERSEN, H.H., 1997 : *The Central Monumental Buildings* (= *Qala'at al-Bahrain* 2 = *JASP* 30/2), Aarhus.

HOFFMANN, I., 1984 : *Der Erlass Telepinus* (= *TH* 11), München.

HOFFNER, H.A., 1975 : « Propaganda and Political Justification in Hittite Historiography » *in* GOEDICKE, H., ROBERTS, J.J.M. (Ed.), *Unity and Diversity. Essays in the History, Literature, and Religion of the Ancient Near East*, Baltimore, London, 49-62.

HORNUNG, E., 1964 : *Untersuchungen zur Chronologie und Geschichte des Neuen Reiches* (= *Ägyptische Abhandlungen* 11), Wiesbaden.

HORSNELL, M., 1974 : *The Year-Names of the First Dynasty of Babylon ; with a Catalogue of the Year-Names from Sumuabum to Samsuiluna*, PhD, University of Toronto.

HUBER, P.J., 1987a : « Dating by Lunar Eclipse Omina with Speculations on the Birth of Omen Astrology » *in* BERGGREN, J.L., GOLDSTEIN, B.R. (Ed.), *From Ancient Omens to Statistical Mechanics. Essays on the Exact Sciences Presented to Asger Aaboe* (= *Acta Historica Scientiarum Naruralium et Medicinalium* 39), Copenhague, 3-13.

HUBER, P.J., 1987b : « Astronomical Evidence for the Long and Against the Middle and Short Chronologies » *in* ÅSTRÖM, P. (Ed.), *High, Middle or Low? Acts of an International Colloquium on Absolute Chronolgy Held at the University of Gothenburg 20th-22nd August 1987*. Part 1, Gothenburg, 5-17.

HUBER *et al.* 1982 = HUBER, P.J., SACHS, A., STOL, M., WHITING, R.M., LEICHTY, E., WALKER, C.B.F., VAN DRIEL, G., 1982 : *Astronomical Dating of Babylon I and Ur III* (= *Monographic Journals of the Near East, Occ. Papers* 1/4), Malibu.

IMAN JAMIL AL-UBAID, 1983 : *Unpublished Cuneiform Texts from Old Babylonian Period, Diyala Region, Tell Muhammad.* MA Thesis, University of Baghdad (Arabic).

INVERNIZZI, A., 1980 : « Excavations in the Yelkhi Area (Hamrin Project, Iraq) », *Mesopotamia* 15, 19-49.

ITT 2 = DE GENOUILLAC, H., 1910-11

JACOBSEN, T., 1939a: *Cuneiform Texts in the National Museum, Copenhagen, Chiefly of Economical Contents*, Leiden.

JACOBSEN, T., 1939b : *The Sumerian King List* (= *AS* 11), Chicago.

JACOBSEN, T., 1940 : « Historical Data » *in* FRANKFORT, H., LLOYD, S., JACOBSEN, T., *The Gimilsin Temple and the Palace of the Rulers at Tell Asmar* (= *OIP* 43), Chicago, 116-200 and 244.

JACOBSEN, T., 1953 : « The Reign of Ibbī-Suen », *JCS* 7, 36-47.

JANSSEN *et al.* 1994 = JANSSEN, C., GASCHE, H., TANRET, M., 1994 : « Du chantier à la tablette. Ur-Utu et l'histoire de sa maison à Sippar-Amnānum » *in* GASCHE, H. *et al.* (Ed.), *Cinquante-deux réflexions sur le Proche-Orient ancien offertes en hommage à Léon De Meyer* (= *MHEO* 2), Leuven, 91-123.

JOANNÈS, F., 1992: « Histoire de Harâdum à l'époque paléo-babylonienne » *in* KEPINSKI-LECOMTE, C. (Ed.), *Haradum* 1. *Une ville nouvelle sur le Moyen-Euphrate (XVIII*e*-XVII*e *siècles av. J.-C.)*, Paris, 30-36.

JORDAN, J., 1930 : « Der Innin-Tempel Karaïndaschs », *UVB* 1, 30-38.

KAJ = EBELING, E., 1927

KAR 2 = EBELING, E., 1923

KARSTENS, K., 1981 : « Nordabschnitt II, nördlicher Teil 1975-1977 » *in* HROUDA, B. (Ed.), *Isin-Išān Baḥrīyāt* 2 (= *ABAW* NF 87), München, 27-48.

KAV = SCHROEDER, O., 1920

KEISER, C.E., 1971 : *Neo-Sumerian Account Texts from Drehem* (= *BIN* 3), New Haven, London.

KEPINSKI-LECOMTE, C., 1992 : « Introduction » *in* KEPINSKI-LECOMTE, C. (Ed.), *Haradum* I. *Une ville nouvelle sur le Moyen-Euphrate (XVIII*e*-XVII*e *siècles av. J.C.)*, Paris, 9-10.

KHANZADYAN, E., 1983 : « A XVIth Cent. Babylonian Weight-Stone with a Cuneiform Inscription from the Metsamor Excavations. 1. The Circumstances of Recovery of the Weight », *Drevnij Vostok* 4, 113-117 (Russian ; English summary, 295-296).

KIENAST, B., 1965 : « Zu einigen Datenformeln aus der frühen Isinzeit », *JCS* 19, 45-55.

KLENGEL, H., 1983 : *Altbabylonische Texte aus Babylon* (= *VS* 22), Berlin.

KNUDTZON, J.A., 1915 : *Die El-Amarna-Tafeln* 1-2 (= *VAB* 2), Leipzig (Anmerkungen und Register bearbeitet von O. Weber und E. Ebeling).

KUNIHOLM, P.I., 1993: « A Date-List for Bronze Age and Iron Age Monuments Based on Combined Dendrochronological and Radiocarbon Evidence » *in* MELLINK, M., PORADA, E., ÖZGÜÇ, T. (Ed.), *Aspects of Art and Iconography : Anatolia and its Neighbors. Studies in Honor of Nimet Özgüç*, Ankara, 371-373.

KUNIHOLM *et al.* 1996 = KUNIHOLM, P.I., KROMER, B., MANNING, S.W., NEWTON, M., LATINI, C.E., BRUCE, M.J., 1996: « Anatolian Tree Rings and the Absolute Chronology of the Eastern Mediterranean, 2220-718 BC », *Nature* 381, 780-783.

LÆSSØE, J., 1965 : « IM 62100 : A Letter from Tell Shemshara », *AS* 16, 189-196.

LAFONT, B., 1994 : « L'avènement de Shu-Sîn », *RA* 88, 97-119.

LANDSBERGER, B., 1949 : « Jahreszeiten im Sumerisch-Akkadischen », *JNES* 8, 248-272.

LANDSBERGER, B., 1954: « Assyrische Königsliste und 'dunkles Zeitalter' », *JCS* 8, 31-73, 106-133.

LARSEN, M.T., 1976 : *The Old Assyrian City-State and its Colonies* (= *Mesopot. C.* 4), Copenhagen.

LASKAR, J., 1994 : « The Stability of the Solar System » *in* GURZADYAN, V.G., PFENNIGER, D. (Ed.), *Ergodic Concepts in Stellar Dynamics*, Berlin, Heidelberg, 112-118.

LEEMANS, W.F., 1960 : *Foreign Trade in the Old Babylonian Period as Revealed by Texts from Southern Mesopotamia* (= *SDIOA* 6), Leiden.

LIAGRE BÖHL : see DE LIAGRE BÖHL

LUTZ, H.F., 1931 : *Legal and Economic Documents from Ashjâli* (= *UCPSP* 10/1), Berkeley.

MANNING, S.W., 1995 : *The Absolute Chronology of the Aegean Early Bronze Age : Archaeology, Radiocarbon and History* (= *Monographs in Mediterranean Archaeology* 1), Sheffield.

MATTHEWS, D.M., 1990 : *Principles of Composition in Near Eastern Glyptic of the Later Second Millennium BC* (= *OBOSA* 8), Göttingen, Freiburg.

McCOWN, D.E., HAINES, R.C., 1967 : *Nippur* I. *Temple of Enlil, Scribal Quarter, and Soundings* (= *OIP* 78), Chicago.

MDP 47 = GASCHE, H., 1973

MHEM 1 = GASCHE, H., 1989

MICHAEL, H.N., RALPH, E.K. (Ed.), 1973 : *Dating Techniques for the Archaeologist*, Cambridge MA, London (second print.).

MICHALOWSKI, P., 1977a : « The Death of Šulgi », *Or* NS 46, 220-225.

MICHALOWSKI, P., 1977b : « Dūrum and Uruk during the Ur III Period », *Mesopotamia* 12, 83-96.

MILLARD, A.R., 1994 : *The Eponyms of the Assyrian Empire, 910-612 BC* (= *State Archives of Assyria Studies* 2), Helsinki.

MINSAER, K., 1991 : « La poterie du chantier E3 », *NAPR* 6, 41-71.

MORAN, W.L., 1992 : *The Amarna Letters*, Baltimore.

NA'AMAN, N., 1984 : « Statements of Time-Spans by Babylonian and Assyrian Kings and Mesopotamian Chronology », *Iraq* 46, 115-123.

NAPR 3 : PONS 1989

NAPR 6 : MINSAER 1991

NASSOUHI, E., 1927 : « Grande liste des rois d'Assyrie », *AfO* 4, 1-11.

NEUGEBAUER, O., 1967 : « Problems and Methods in Babylonian Mathematical Astronomy. Henry Norris Russel Lecture, 1967 », *Astronomical Journal* 72, 964-972.

NEUGEBAUER, O., 1975 : *A History of Ancient Mathematical Astronomy*, New York, Heidelberg, Berlin.

NEUGEBAUER, O., 1983a : *Astronomy and History. Selected Essays*, New York, Heidelberg, Berlin.

NEUGEBAUER, O., 1983b [1955] : *Astronomical Cuneiform Texts. Babylonian Ephemerides of the Seleucid Period for the Motion of the Sun, the Moon, and the Planets* 2 (= *Sources in the History of Mathematics and Physical Sciences* 5), New York, Heidelberg, Berlin.

NEWHALL *et al.*, 1983 = NEWHALL, X.X., STANDISH, E.M., WILLIAMS, J.G., 1983 : « DE 102 : A Numerically Integrated Ephemeris of the Moon and Planets Spanning Forty-Four Centuries », *Astronomy and Astrophysics* 125, 150-167.

NEWTON, R., 1976 : *Ancient Planetary Observations and the Validity of Ephemeris Time*, Baltimore.

NEWTON, R., 1977 : *The Crime of Claudius Ptolemy*, Baltimore.

OIP 78 = McCOWN, D.E., HAINES, R.C., 1967

PARPOLA, S., 1993 : *Letters from Assyrian and Babylonian Scholars* (= *SAA* 10), Helsinki.

PARROT, A., 1968a : « Les fouilles de Larsa. Deuxième et troisième campagnes (1967) », *Syria* 45, 205-237.

PARROT, A., 1968b : « Fouilles de Larsa (Senkereh) 1967 », *Sumer* 24, 39-44.

PEDERSÉN, O., 1985 : *Archives and Libraries in the City of Assur. A Survey of the Material from the German Excavations*, Part 1 (= *Acta Universitatis Upsaliensis. Studia Semitica Upsaliensia* 6), Uppsala.

PINCHES, T.G., 1880 : *The Cuneiform Inscriptions of Western Asia* 5. *A Selection from the Miscellaneous Inscriptions of Assyria and Babylonia, prepared ... by ... Sir H.C. Rawlinson*, London.

POEBEL, A., 1942a : « The Assyrian King List from Khorsabad », *JNES* 1, 247-306.

POEBEL, A., 1942b : « The Assyrian King List from Khorsabad — Concluded », *JNES* 1, 460-492.

POEBEL, A., 1943 : « The Assyrian King List from Khorsabad — Concluded », *JNES* 2, 56-90.

PONS, N., 1989 : « Tell ed-Dēr 1988. Un quartier du 17e siècle avant notre ère (Rapport préliminaire). 2. La poterie et les tombes du chantier F », *NAPR* 3, 19-25.

PORADA, E., 1975 : « Iranische Kunst » *in* ORTHMANN, W., (Ed.), *Der alte Orient* (= *Propyläen Kunstgeschichte* 14), Berlin, 363-398.

POSTGATE, J.N., 1991 : « The Chronology of Assyria — An Insurmountable Obstacle », *Cambridge Archaeological Journal* 1, 244-246.

QUINTANA, E., 1996 : « Le sukkalmah Kuknasur », *NABU* 86).

RANKE, H., 1906 : *Babylonian Legal and Business Documents from the Time of the First Dynasty of Babylon, Chiefly from Sippar* (*BE* VI/1), Philadelphia.

REINER, E., PINGREE, D., 1975 : *Babylonian Planetary Omens. Part 1 : The Venus Tablet of Ammiṣaduqa* (= *BiMes* 2/1), Malibu.

REUTHER, O., 1926 : *Die Innenstadt von Babylon (Merkes)* (= *WVDOG* 47), Leipzig.

RIMB 2 = FRAME, G., 1995

ROCHBERG-HALTON, F., 1988 : *Aspects of Babylonian Celestial Divination. The Lunar Eclipse Tablets of Enūma Anu Enlil* (= *AfO Beih.* 22), Horn.

ROUAULT, O., SAPORETTI, C., 1985 : « Old Babylonian Texts from Tell Yelkhi (Hamrīn Project, Iraq) », *Mesopotamia* 20, 23-52.

ROWTON, M.B., 1946 : « Mesopotamian Chronology and the 'Era of Menophres' », *Iraq* 8, 94-110.

ROWTON, M.B., 1951 : « *Ṭuppu* and the Date of Hammurabi », *JNES* 10, 184-204.

ROWTON, M.B., 1959a : « The Background of the Treaty between Ramses II and Ḫattušiliš III », *JCS* 13, 1-11.

ROWTON, M.B., 1959b : « *Ṭuppū* in the Assyrian King-Lists », *JNES* 18, 213-221.

ROWTON, M.B., 1976 [1970] : « Chronology. II. Ancient Western Asia » *in* EDWARDS, I.E.S, GADD, C.J, HAMMOND, N.G.L. (Ed.), *The Cambridge Ancient History*³ I/1, Cambridge, 193-239.

SAA 10 = PARPOLA, S., 1993

SAPORETTI, C., 1979 : *Gli eponimi medio-assiri* (= *BiMes* 9), Malibu.

SARKISYAN, G., DIAKONOFF, I., 1983 : « A XVIth Cent. Babylonian Weight-Stone with a Cuneiform Inscription from the Metsamor Excavations. 2. The Cuneiform Inscription on the Weight », *Drevnij Vostok* 4, 117-122 (Russian ; English summary, 296-297).

SARRE, F., HERZFELD, E., 1920 : *Archäologische Reise im Euphrat- und Tigris-Gebiet* 2, Berlin.

SASSMANNSHAUSEN, L., 1994 : « Ein ungewöhnliches mittelbabylonisches Urkundenfragment aus Nippur », *BaM* 25, 447-457.

SCHEIL, V., 1900 : *Textes élamites-sémitiques (Première série)* (= *MDP* 2), Paris.

SCHEIL, V., 1902 : *Textes élamites sémitiques (Deuxième série)* (= *MDP* 4), Paris.

SCHEIL, V., 1905 : *Textes élamites-sémitiques (Troisième série)* (= *MDP* 6), Paris.

SCHEIL, V. (in collab. with J.E. Gautier), 1908 : *Textes élamites-sémitiques (Quatrième série)* (= *MDP* 10), Paris.

SCHEIL, V., 1913 : *Textes élamites-sémitiques (Cinquième série)* (= *MDP* 14), Paris.

SCHEIL, V., 1930 : *Actes juridiques susiens* (= *MDP* 22), Paris.

SCHEIL, V., 1932 : *Actes juridiques susiens (Suite : n° 166 à n° 327)* (= *MDP* 23), Paris.

SCHEIL, V., 1933 : *Actes juridiques susiens (Suite : n° 328 à n° 395). Inscriptions des achéménides (Supplément et suite)* (= *MDP* 24), Paris.

SCHEIL, V., 1939 : *Mélanges épigraphiques* (= *MDP* 28), Paris.

SCHOTT, A, 1930 : « Die inschriftlichen Quellen zur Geschichte Ēannas », *UVB* 1, 45-67.

SCHROEDER, O., 1920 : *Keilschrifttexte aus Assur verschiedenen Inhalts* (= *WVDOG* 35), Leipzig.

SCHUBERT, K., 1948 : « Die altorientalischen Dynastien zur Zeit Hammurapis von Babylon », *WZKM* 51, 21-33.

SIGRIST, M., 1988 : *Isin Year Names* (= *Institute of Archaeology Publications, Assyriological Series* 2), Berrien Springs, Michigan.

SIGRIST, M., 1990 : *Larsa Year Names* (= *Institute of Archaeology Publications, Assyriological Series* 3), Berrien Springs, Michigan.

SIGRIST, M., 1995 : *Neo-Sumerian Texts from the Royal Ontario Museum* 1. *The Administration at Drehem*, Bethesda.

SIGRIST, M., GOMI, T., 1991 : *The Comprehensive Catalogue of Published Ur III Tablets*, Bethesda, Maryland.

SKAIST, A., 1994 : *The Old Babylonian Loan Contract. Its History and Geography*, Ramat Gan.

SKL = JACOBSEN, T., 1939b

SMITH, S., 1945 : « Middle Minoan I - II and Babylonian Chronology », *AJA* 49, 1-24.

SOLLBERGER, E., 1954-56 : « Sur la chronologie des rois d'Ur et quelques problèmes connexes », *AfO* 17, 10-48.

SOLLBERGER, E., 1965 : *Royal Inscriptions. Part II* (= *UET* 8), London.

STEINKELLER, P., 1988 : « On the Identity of the Toponym LÚ.SU(A) », *JAOS* 108, 197-202.

STEPHENSON, F.R., 1996 : *in* « Current Issues in Archaeoastronomy, Royal Astron. Society Specialist Discussion Meeting, London », *Observatory* 116, 282-283.

STEPHENSON, F.R., SAID, S.S., 1989 : « Non-Tidal Changes in the Earth's Rate of Rotation as Deduced from Medieval Solar Eclipses », *Astronomy and Astrophysics* 215, 181-189.

STEPHENSON, F.R., YAU, K.K., 1992 : « The Total Solar Eclipse of AD 1221 and the Rotation of the Earth », *Astronomy and Astrophysics* 260, 485-488.

STEVE, M.-J., 1994 : « Suse : la couche XII du Chantier 'A' de la 'Ville Royale' et la fin de l'époque des sukkalmah » *in* GASCHE, H. *et al.* (Ed.), *Cinquante-deux réflexions sur le Proche-Orient ancien offertes en hommage à Léon De Meyer* (= *MHEO* 2), Leuven, 23-30.

STEVE, M.-J., VALLAT, F., 1989 : « La dynastie des Igihalkides : nouvelles interprétations », *AIO* I, 223-238.

STEVE *et al.* 1980 = STEVE, M.-J., GASCHE, H., DE MEYER, L., 1980 : « La Susiane au deuxième millénaire : à propos d'une interprétation des fouilles de Suse » (with an Annex by P. AMIET), *IrAnt* 15, 49-154.

STOL, M., 1976 : *Studies in Old Babylonian History* (= *UNHAI* 40), Leiden.

STOLPER, M.W., 1982 : « On the dynasty of Šimaški and the Early Sukkalmahs », *ZA* 72, 42-67.

STONE, E.C., 1977 : « Economic Crisis and Social Upheaval in Old Babylonian Nippur » *in* LEVINE D., YOUNG, T.C. Jr., (Ed.), *Mountains and Lowlands : Essays in the Archaeology of Greater Mesopotamia* (= *BiMes* 7), Malibu, 267-289.

STONE, E.C., 1987 : *Nippur Neighborhoods* (= *SAOC* 44), Chicago.

STRASSMAIER, J.N., 1890 : *Inschriften von Cambyses, König von Babylon* (= *BT* 8-9), Leipzig.

SYKES, K.L., 1973 : « The Year Names of the Ur III Period », M.A. Thesis, University of Chicago.

TADMOR, H., 1958 : « Historical Implications of the Correct Rendering of Akkadian *dâku* », *JNES* 17, 129-141.

TAHA BAQIR, 1945 : *Iraq Government Excavations at ʿAqar Qūf. Second Interim Report 1943-1944* (= *Iraq*, Suppl. 1945), London.

TAHA BAQIR, 1948 : « A Date-list of Ishbi-Irra », *Sumer* 4, 103-114.

TAHA BAQIR, 1949 : « Date-Formulae & Date-Lists from Harmal », *Sumer* 5, 34-38.

TCL 6 = THUREAU-DANGIN, F., 1922

TD 2 : GASCHE, H., 1978

THUREAU-DANGIN, F., 1922 : *Tablettes d'Uruk à l'usage des prêtres du temple d'Anu au temps des Seleucides* (= *TCL* 6), Paris.

TIM 5 = VAN DIJK, J.J.A., 1968

TOOMER, G.J., 1984 : *Ptolemy's Almagest*, London.

UCPSP 10/1 = LUTZ, H.F., 1931

UET 1 = GADD *et al.* 1928

UNGNAD, A., 1909 : « Zur Geschichte der Nachbarstaaten Babyloniens zur Zeit der Hammurapi-Dynastie », *BA* 6/5, 1-11.

UNGNAD, A., 1938a : « Datenlisten », *RlA* 2, 131-194.

UNGNAD, A., 1938b : « Eponymen », *RlA* 2, 412-457.

VALLAT, F., 1990 : « Réflexions sur l'époque des *sukkalmah* » *in* VALLAT, F. (Ed.), *Contribution à l'histoire de l'Iran. Mélanges offerts à Jean Perrot*, Paris, 119-127.

VALLAT, F., 1993 : « Kuk-Našur et Ammiṣaduqa », *NABU* 39).

VALLAT, F., 1994 : « Succession royale en Elam au IIème millénaire » *in* GASCHE, H. *et al.* (Ed.), *Cinquante-deux réflexions sur le Proche-Orient ancien offertes en hommage à Léon De Meyer* (= *MHEO* 2), Leuven, 1-14.

VALLAT, F., 1996a : « Šu-ilišu, Iddin-Dagan et Imazu, roi d'Anšan », *NABU* 87).

VALLAT, F., 1996b : « L'Elam à l'époque paléo-babylonienne et ses rapports avec la Mésopotamie » *in* DURAND, J.-M. (Ed.), *Amurru* I. *Mari, Ebla et les Hourrites, dix ans de travaux*, Paris, 297-319.

VALLAT, F., 1997a : « La date du règne de Gudea », *NABU* 37).

VALLAT, F., 1997b : « Nouveaux problèmes de succession en Elam », *IrAnt* 32, 53-70.

VALLAT, F., 1997c : « Les trois Kuk-Našur », *NABU* 110).

VAN AS, A., JACOBS, L., 1987 : « Second Millenium B.C. Goblet Bases from Tell ed-Deir — The Relationship Between Form and Technique » *in* VAN AS, A. (Ed), *A Knapsack full of Pottery, Archaeo-Ceramological Miscellanea dedicated to H.J. Franken on the Occasion of his Seventieth Birthday. July 4, 1987* (= *Newsletter* 5), Leiden, 39-53.

VAN AS, A., JACOBS, L., 1988 : « Report on the Activities of the Working Group on Mesopotamian Pottery During the Years 1987-1988 », *Newsletter* 6, 1-22.

VAN DE MIEROOP, M., 1987 : *Sumerian Administrative Documents from the Reigns of Išbi-Erra and Šu-ilišu* (= *BIN* 10), New Haven.

VAN DER MEER, P., 1963 : *The Chronology of Ancient Western Asia and Egypt* (= *DMOA* 2), Leiden (second, rev. ed.).

VAN DER WAERDEN, B.L., 1957 : « Babylonische Planetenrechnung », *Vierteljahrsschrift der Naturforschenden Gesellschaft in Zürich* 102/2, 39-60.

VAN DIJK, J.J.A., 1968 : *Cuneiform Texts. Old Babylonian Contracts and Related Material* (= *TIM* 5), Wiesbaden.

VAN DIJK, J.J.A., 1978 : « Išbi'Erra, Kindattu, l'homme d'Elam, et la chute de la ville d'Ur », *JCS* 30, 189-207.

VAN DIJK, J.J.A., 1986 : « Die dynastischen Heiraten zwischen Kassiten und Elamern : eine verhängnisvolle Politik », *Or* NS 55, 159-170.

VAN ESS, M., 1988 : « Keramik von der Akkad- bis zum Ende der altbabylonischen Zeit aus den Planquadraten N XV und XVI und aus dem Sînkāšid-Palast in Uruk-Warka », *BaM* 19, 321-442.

VEENHOF, K.R., 1985 : « Eponyms of the 'Later Old Assyrian Period' and Mari Chronology », *MARI* 4, 191-218.

VON BECKERATH, J., 1992 : « Das Kalendarium des Papyrus Ebers und die Chronologie des ägyptischen Neuen Reiches. Gegenwärtiger Stand der Frage », *Ägypten und Levante* 21, 23-27.

VON BECKERATH, J., 1997 : *Chronologie des pharaonischen Ägypten. Die Zeitbestimmung der ägyptischen Geschichte von der Vorzeit bis 332 v. Chr.* (= *Münchner Ägyptologische Studien* 46), Mainz.

WALKER, C.B.F., 1978 : « Texts and Fragments », *JCS* 30, 234-250.

WALKER, C.B.F., WILCKE, C., 1981 : « Preliminary Report on the Inscriptions, Autumn 1975, Spring 1977, Autumn 1978 » *in* HROUDA, B. (Ed.), *Isin-Išān Baḫrīyāt* 2 (= *ABAW* NF 87), München, 91-102.

WALL-ROMANA, C., 1990 : « An Areal Location of Agade », *JNES* 49, 205-245.

WATERMAN, L., 1916 : *Business Documents of the Hammurapi Period from the British Museum*, London.

WEIDNER, E.F., 1923 : *Politische Dokumente aus Kleinasien. Die Staatsverträge in akkadischer Sprache aus dem Archiv von Boghazköi* (= *BoSt* 8), Leipzig.

WEIDNER, E.F., 1935-36 : « Aus den Tagen eines assyrischen Schattenkönigs », *AfO* 10, 1-52.

WEIDNER, E.F., 1945-51 : « Bemerkungen zur Königsliste aus Chorsābād », *AfO* 15, 85-102

WEIDNER, E.F., 1954-56 : « Die astrologische Serie Enûma Anu Enlil », *AfO* 17, 71-89.

WEIDNER, E.F., 1957-71 : « Gandaš », *RlA* 3, 138-139.

WEISSBACH, F.H., 1903 : *Babylonische Miscellen* (= *WVDOG* 4), Leipzig.

WHITING, R.M., 1990 : « Tell Leilan / Šubat-Enlil. Chronological Problems and Perspectives » *in* EICHLER, S., WÄFLER, M., WARBURTON, D. (Ed.), *Tall al-Ḥamīdīya* 2 (= *OBOSA* 6), Freiburg, Göttingen, 167-218.

WHITING, R.M., 1994 : « The Post-Canonical and Extra-Canonical Eponyms » *in* MILLARD, A., *The Eponyms of the Assyrian Empire, 910-612 BC* (= *State Archives of Assyria Studies* 2), Helsinki, 72-78.

WILCKE, C., 1987 : « 5. Die Inschriftenfunde der 7. und 8. Kampagnen (1983 und 1984) » *in* HROUDA, B. (Ed.), *Isin-Išān Baḫrīyāt* 3 (= *ABAW* NF 94), München, 83-120.

WOOLLEY, C.L., MALLOWAN, M., 1976 : *The Old Babylonian Period* (= *UE* 7), London, Philadelphia.

YOS 1 = CLAY, A.T., 1915

YOS 10 = GOETZE, A., 1947

ZETTLER, R.L., 1993 : *Nippur* III : *Kassite Buildings in Area WC-1* (= *OIP* 111), Chicago.

D/1998/0634/1 (Belgium)
ISBN 1-885923-10-4 (USA)

Library of Congress Catalog Card Number : 98-84354

Printed in Belgium